healthy entertaining

healthy
entertaining

KYLE BOOKS

This edition published in 2004 by Kyle Books,
an imprint of Kyle Cathie Limited.
general.enquiries@kyle-cathie.com
www.kylecathie.com

Distributed by National Book Network
4501 Forbes Blvd., Suite 200
Lanham, MD 20706
Phone: (301) 459 3366
Fax: (301) 429 5746

ISBN 1-904920-07-1

The Library of Congress Cataloguing-in-Publication
Data is available on file.

Printed and bound in China by C & C Offset
Printing Co., Ltd.

contents

introduction

Today's entertaining focuses on providing simple, fresh food to nourish our friends and family. We no longer feel the need to spend hours on end slaving over a hot stove to impress our friends with the latest in food fashions. Eating should be a pleasure, not a competitive sport.

Dinner parties don't need to be an excuse for a complete blow-out either. Many people these days are more health- and weight-conscious, and the recipes in this book demonstrate that you can serve fresh and healthy food to your friends and family without breaking the basics of healthy eating. Nutritional information is given for each recipe so you can easily mix and match to put together a healthy menu.

Many of the recipes in this book are quick and easy to prepare and are perfect for weeknight entertaining when time may be short. Others take longer to prepare and are best reserved for occasions when you have a little more time. Recipes that require marinating can either be prepared in the morning before setting off for work, or made up the night before and left in the fridge for 24 hours. In the evening all you will have to do is fish it out of the marinade and cook it. Desserts such as sorbets can be made several days in advance and kept in the freezer.

The secret of stress-free entertaining is planning. If you haven't got a lot of experience in the kitchen, keep it simple and don't attempt to cook anything too complicated, or something you've not cooked before. Do the shopping the night before, giving you a chance to pick up any ingredients you may not have been able to find on the day itself.

If it's to be a formal occasion, set the table in the morning before you go to work and don't forget to put the wine in the fridge to chill.

Menu-planning is mainly common sense, but it's better to follow a few principles to avoid potential pitfalls. In general, it's easier to select a main course then choose a starter and dessert to complement. When planning your menu, variety and balance are key. Think of the ingredients, cooking method, and colour of the dishes you plan to serve. Don't serve eggs in every course, or three fried dishes, or an all-white plate - think chicken breast, cauliflower, and mashed potato – just replacing the cauliflower with carrot will make the food look much more attractive.

Similarly, don't serve three courses that all need be cooked on the night. If you're planning on a stir-fry which needs to be prepared at the last minute, choose a salad as an appetizer and a sorbet for dessert - that way you'll lower not only your stress levels but also the amount of time you need to spend in the kitchen.

If you get frustrated being in the kitchen while everyone else is enjoying drinks in the next room, choose dishes that need no last-minute preparation, such as a casserole. That way you can prepare everything beforehand and pop it in the oven before your guests arrive, leaving you to give your full attention to your guests. Choose a cold dessert - ice cream or sorbet, for example, and that will cut down even further on the time you need to spend in the kitchen on the night. If on the other hand you do your entertaining in the kitchen you can choose dishes that need last-minute attention and turn the cooking into a communal activity.

tips & shortcuts

dinner party planning

To make sure your dinner party goes without a hitch, it can be a good idea to check if your guests have any dietary restrictions, food allergies, or special needs before starting to plan your menu. Peanuts, strawberries, and seafood are some of the most common causes of food allergy so avoid these altogether in the whole meal if any of your guests are affected. Vegetarians come in different 'varieties' - check whether your guests eat fish or dairy products before planning the meal. There are plenty of vegetarian and even vegan dishes that even the most ardent of meat-eaters will enjoy. Pork, seafood, and alcohol may all pose problems for religious reasons. If in doubt, simply ask your guests.

be creative

If you're planning a barbecue, don't automatically reach for the beefburgers and sausages. Prepared convenience foods tend to be higher in fat and salt than most home-cooked food. Fish and vegetable skewers are quick and easy to prepare and are lower in fat than many traditional barbecue foods. Complement with a couple of salads and some baked potatoes for a balanced meal.

nibbles

If you're serving nibbles before dinner, replace the usual peanuts and potato chips with some crudités and a low-fat cream cheese dip. Batons of carrots and cucumber, slices of pepper, cherry tomatoes, and florets of cauliflower look attractive arranged on a large plate and won't pile on the calories.

how to use this book

Each recipe provides information about the number of servings it provides, and how long it takes to prepare and cook. As a general principle, the preparation time is the time it takes to wash, prepare, and chop the ingredients for the recipe, and the cooking time is the time you actually need to spend cooking, although for much of this time the dish may be able to be left to its own devices while you get on with something else.

In addition, each recipe provides nutritional information. As a rough guide, children, sedentary women, and older adults need approximately 1,600 calories per day. Teenage girls, active women, and sedentary men need 2,200 calories, and teenage boys, active men, and very active women need up to 2,800 per day. Current advice is that no more than 10-30 percent of our daily energy intake should come from fats. Most of us should be trying to cut down on total fats, and particularly saturated fats.

Carbohydrates are an important part of everyone's diet. It is recommended that at least a third of our daily intake is made up of starchy foods such as potatoes, yams, wholegrain bread, pasta, noodles, chapattis, rice, sweet potatoes, and so on.

It is recommended that our daily salt intake not exceed 6g. Most of us consume more like 9g (the equivalent of 2 teaspoonfuls). Much of the salt we consume comes from processed convenience foods, but approximately 10 percent of it comes from salt we add to our food, either during cooking or at the table. High salt consumption is implicated in raised blood pressure, which is turn has been linked to a higher risk of heart disease and stroke. There is evidence that the fiber contained in wholegrain foods and in fruit and vegetables may protect against developing some forms of heart disease and cancer.

simple
appetizers
&
suppers

roasted **beetroot &** orange 'latte'

4 fresh small beetroots, trimmed and peeled
1 tablespoon shelled pistachio nuts
grated rind and juice of 4 oranges
1/3 cup milk
1 small wedge honeydew melon, pitted

Preheat the oven to 375°F. Wrap the beetroot in a loose pouch of aluminum foil, sealing the top tightly. Place on a roasting tin and roast for 30-40 minutes until completely tender.

Heat a small skillet. Add the pistachio nuts and cook for a couple of minutes until toasted and lightly brown, shaking the pan occasionally to prevent them from burning.

Remove the beetroots from the oven and tip the contents of the aluminum foil pouch into a food processor or blender. Blend to a purée, then with the machine still running, slowly pour in the orange juice and add half of the rind. Finally, pour in two thirds of the milk until just combined.

Switch off the machine and season to taste. Pour into heatproof glasses and sprinkle the toasted pistachios on top. Froth the remaining milk using a cappuccino steamer or whisk and then carefully spoon on top of the beetroot mixture. Sprinkle over the remaining orange rind and pare shavings of the melon on top to serve.

TIP

Having a cappuccino maker helps for this recipe but don't worry if you don't have access to one. There are now a number of decent gadgets available in cookshops which do a perfectly adequate job.

Nutritional value per serving:

Calories: 96

Fats: 2g

Carbohydrates: 17g

Salt: 0.25g

Saturated fat: 0.4g

Fiber: 2.4g

oyster salad

2 dozen oysters, shucked and roughly chopped

2 yellow or green chiles, pitted and
   finely chopped

2-3 scallions, trimmed and roughly chopped

4 tablespoons lime or lemon juice or white
   wine vinegar

salt

To serve

chopped cilantro

pickled chiles

quartered limes or lemons

Combine all the ingredients, leave to marinate for 3-4 hours, drain, spoon back into the shells or glass bowls, dress with freshly chopped cilantro and serve well-chilled, with pickled chiles and quartered limes.

How to open oysters

Fold up a dish towel and place on the palm of your hand for protection. With the flat side of the oyster uppermost and the pointed end facing towards you, slide the point of an oyster knife between the two shells to sever the nerve holding the oyster closed. Remove the top shell and discard. Slide the knife under the oyster in the shell to cut it loose from the bottom shell. Remove the oyster, or leave in the shell if serving whole.

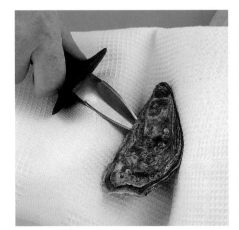 

Nutritional value per serving:

Calories: 51

Fats: 1g

Carbohydrates: 2g

Salt: 1.22g

Saturated fat: 0.2g

Fiber: 0.1g

mixed ceviche

8oz salmon fillets

8oz white fish fillets

8oz mackerel fillets

juice and rind of 4 limes

juice and rind of 2 lemons

juice of 1 orange

1 tablespoon white wine vinegar

2 medium unpeeled potatoes (preferably a waxy
   salad variety), sliced into $\frac{1}{4}$ in thick discs

5 tablespoons extra-virgin olive oil

bunch of chives, finely chopped

4 handfuls of mixed salad leaves

salt and freshly-ground pepper

Well ahead, ideally the day before: cut the fish into strips about $\frac{3}{4}$in thick and place in a bowl. Sprinkle with the juice and rind from the limes, lemons, and orange, together with the vinegar. Cover and refrigerate for 6 hours, or preferably overnight.

Boil the potatoes in boiling salted water until just tender, drain and refresh in cold water, but try to keep them slightly warm. Pile the potato slices in the center of 4 plates. Drizzle over a little olive oil and season with salt and pepper. Strain the fish, reserving the citrus juices, and scatter the pieces around the potatoes. Sprinkle over the chives and top with the salad leaves.

Combine a dessertspoon of the reserved citrus juices with 3 tablespoons of olive oil, season with salt and pepper and pour over the salad leaves to serve.

How to skin fish fillets

Put the fillet of fish skin-side down onto a chopping board. With the knife at 45° angle, cut through the flesh down onto the skin at the tail end. Hold on to the skin and half push, half saw the flesh off the skin. Use the skins for fish stock.

Nutritional value per serving:

Calories: 465

Fats: 30g

Carbohydrates: 15g

Salt: 0.52g

Saturated fat: 5g

Fiber: 1.1g

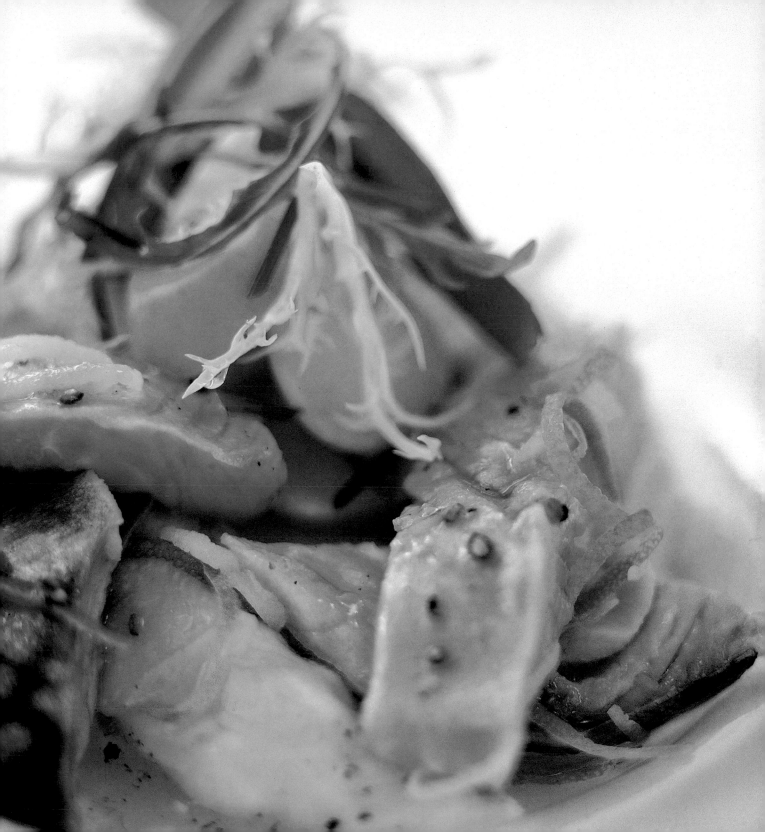

peruvian ceviche

2lb fillets of cod, sole, flounder or scallops

4 limes

2 lemons

2 garlic cloves, finely chopped

fresh cilantro, chopped

1-2 fresh chiles

1 small onion, finely sliced

1 green bell pepper, finely diced

1 red bell pepper, finely diced

salt and freshly-ground black pepper

To serve

crisp lettuce leaves

5-6 scallions

sweetcorn, optional

2 avocados

diced bell peppers

Skin the fish; slice or cube into $\frac{1}{2}$in pieces and put into a deep stainless steel or china bowl. Squeeze the juice from the limes and lemons and pour over the fish. Sprinkle with salt, pepper and garlic. Cover and leave to marinate for 2-3 hours in the fridge.

Next add the fresh cilantro, onions, chiles and the red and green bell peppers. Cover and leave for $2\frac{1}{2}$ hours in the fridge. Then serve or keep covered until later.

To serve: arrange a few crisp lettuce leaves on a plate and place a tablespoon of ceviche in the center. Decorate with slices of avocado, diced bell peppers, sweetcorn, and scallions. Serve it with crusty white bread or tortillas.

Nutritional value per serving:

Calories: 133

Fats: 6g

Carbohydrates: 5g

Salt: 0.34g

Saturated fat: 0.8g

Fiber: 2g

crab & avocado towers

2 avocados, skinned, pit removed and cut
   into small dice
juice of 1 lime
3 cups cooked white crabmeat, shell removed
10 plum tomatoes, skinned, pitted and cut into
   small dice (see below)
2 shallots, finely diced
$^1/_4$ cup chopped chives
3 tablespoons lemon-flavored olive oil,
   or extra-virgin olive oil
salt and freshly-ground black pepper

Dressing
2 tablespoons white wine vinegar
1 teaspoon caster sugar
4 tablespoons extra-virgin olive oil
2 tablespoons chopped dill
salt and freshly-ground black pepper

Mix all the ingredients for the dressing.

Line a flat tray with plastic wrap. To assemble the towers: place 10 ring molds, $2^3/_4$ x $1^1/_4$in deep, on the tray. Mix the avocado with the lime juice, season and divide into 10 equal amounts. Spoon into the base of each mold and smooth with the back of a teaspoon. Repeat with the white crab meat. Mix the tomatoes, shallot, chives, and olive oil, season, then layer as before.

With a palette knife or fish slice, place a tower in the center of each plate. Remove the molds carefully. Drizzle the dressing around the plate and serve.

How to skin tomatoes

Cut a cross into the base of each tomato and plunge into a bowl of hot water. Leave for a few minutes until the skins start to wrinkle. The skins will then be easy to peel off.

Nutritional value per serving:

Calories: 194

Fats: 16g

Carbohydrates: 3g

Salt: 0.85g

Saturated fat: 2.1g

Fiber: 1.6g

chili-pickled orange, feta, & olive salad

4 oranges, preferably navel

5 tablespoons white wine vinegar

3 tablespoons caster sugar

1 red chile, thinly sliced into rings

5 tablespoons olive oil

2 tablespoons black olives, pitted

$1^{1}/_{3}$ cups feta, cut into $^{1}/_{2}$in cubes

1 tablespoon chopped fresh oregano or parsley

baby spinach and arugula leaves, to garnish
   (optional)

salt and freshly-ground black pepper

Peel the oranges, being sure to remove all the white pith, and cut them into slices $^{1}/_{4}$in thick. Remove any pips and put the orange slices in a shallow dish. Boil the vinegar and sugar together for 2-3 minutes, add the chile and then pour on to the orange slices. Cover and leave overnight.

The next day, drain off the juices from the pickled oranges into a bowl. Whisk in the olive oil to make a dressing and season with salt and pepper. Arrange the oranges in a serving bowl. Stir the olives, feta, and oregano or parsley into the dressing and sprinkle it over the oranges. Sprinkle with coarsely cracked black pepper, scatter over the spinach and arugula leaves, if using, and serve.

TIP

Haloumi or a firm goat's cheese can be used instead of feta.

Some people like to soak feta cheese in warm water or milk before using. This effectively softens the strong, salty flavor.

Nutritional value per serving:

Calories: 406

Fats: 30g

Carbohydrates: 27g

Salt: 2.23g

Saturated fat: 8.5g

Fiber: 2.1g

beetroot, tomato, & cilantro salad with labna

7 new-season baby beetroot

16-18 red cherry tomatoes, halved

8-9 yellow cherry tomatoes, halved

juice of $1/2$ lemon

6 tablespoons virgin olive oil

$1/2$ teaspoon coriander seeds, lightly cracked in a pestle and mortar

cayenne pepper

2 cups fresh cilantro, leaves only

20 small balls of labna cheese

Place the beetroot in a saucepan, cover with cold water and bring to a boil. Reduce the heat to a simmer and cook until they are just tender (alternatively, you could steam them). Drain well and peel. Cut the beetroot into halves or quarters, so they are approximately the same size as the tomatoes. Place the beetroot and tomatoes in a large bowl and add the lemon juice, olive oil, and coriander seeds. Season with salt and a little cayenne and toss the whole lot together. Finally toss in the fresh cilantro leaves, then serve, topped with the balls of labna cheese.

TIP

Labna is a strained yogurt cheese, available from Middle Eastern food shops and some supermarkets. It is easy to make at home: simply strain some thick, Greek-style yogurt through a piece of cheesecloth over a period of two days to drain off the whey, leaving you with a firm yogurt cheese. Roll into small balls between your hands.

Nutritional value per serving:

Calories: 2.54

Fats: 19g

Carbohydrates: 12g

Salt: 0.94g

Saturated fat: 3.6g

Fiber: 2.7g

rice paper wraps with a spicy **soy** dip

5oz sushi-quality tuna (i.e. extremely fresh), the tail end

$^3/_4$ cup snow peas, cut into thin matchsticks

1 medium carrot, cut into thin matchsticks

$^1/_2$ cup Chinese radish, cut into thin matchsticks

1 container cress, cut from base

1 tablespoon sweet soy sauce

juice and rind of 2 limes

1 tablespoon sushi vinegar

8 sheets of rice paper, $8^1/_2$in round

black sesame seeds for garnish

Spicy soy dip

2 tablespoons light soy sauce

1 tablespoon granulated sugar

1 tablespoon sushi vinegar

1 teaspoon gingerroot, peeled and finely chopped

1 garlic clove, finely chopped

2 teaspoons sweet chili sauce

salt and freshly-ground black pepper

Nutritional value per wrap:

Calories: 15

Fats: 0g

Carbohydrates: 2g

Salt: 0.34g

Saturated fat: 0.1g

Fiber: 0.1 g

First prepare all the ingredients. Line a tray with parchment paper. Slice the tuna into wafer-thin discs and set aside. On a separate tray, lay out the vegetables and cress. For the marinade, combine the sweet soy sauce, rind and juice of limes, and sushi vinegar in a bowl. Mix together all the ingredients for the spiced soy dip.

Soak the rice paper in a bowl of cold water for 3-4 minutes until soft. Remove from the water and cut on the diagonal into triangle quarters, laying these on a dish towel so that all the points are facing the same way; season. Dip the tuna in the marinade and place on the rice-paper triangles at the opposite side to the points. Place 3 pieces of each vegetable on the tuna and top with cress. Roll up the rice paper, then place each wrap on a tray lined with a cloth. Cover the wraps with plastic wrap to prevent them drying out. Refrigerate until needed.

To serve, place the wraps on a tray and sprinkle liberally with sesame seeds. Transfer the dip into a small bowl and serve.

TIP

If you do not like tuna, use fresh salmon or cooked shrimp instead.

yellow zucchini & shrimp cous cous

2 cups cous cous

2 cups boiling water

2 tablespoons light olive oil

16 large raw shrimp, de-veined

1 red chile, pitted and finely chopped

1 garlic clove, crushed

4 small yellow zucchini, sliced

2 tablespoons slivered almonds, toasted

4 tablespoons golden raisins

12 black olives

2 tablespoons chopped fresh mint

1 teaspoon chopped preserved salted lemon

salt and freshly-ground black pepper

Dressing

1/2 cup olive oil

juice of 1 lemon

1 garlic clove, crushed

1 tablespoon white wine vinegar

1 tablespoon chopped fresh mint

Place the cous cous in a large bowl, pour over the boiling water, then cover and leave for 5 minutes. Fluff up the cous cous with a fork, then cover again and leave for 5 minutes longer. Fluff up again and season to taste.

Heat the oil in a skillet, add the shrimp, chile, garlic, and zucchini and sauté for 3-4 minutes, until the shrimp and zucchini are cooked. Add the toasted almonds, golden raisins, olives, mint and preserved lemon, then season to taste. Add to the cous cous and toss well together.

Whisk all the ingredients for the dressing together and season to taste. Toss with the cous cous and serve warm.

TIP

Chicken or salmon could be used instead of the prawns.

Preserved lemons can be found in Mediterranean delicatessens.

Nutritional value per serving:

Calories: 612

Fats: 39g

Carbohydrates: 42g

Salt: 1.38g

Saturated fat: 5.1g

Fiber: 1.4g

pastrami-style salmon with herb oil

juice of 2 lemons

³/₄ cup olive oil

4 tablespoons chopped mixed herbs (such as
  dill, cilantro and chervil)

12oz salmon fillet (not from the tail end)

1 tablespoon coriander seeds

3 tablespoons coarse sea salt

grated rind of 1 lemon

2 tablespoons Dijon mustard

¹/₂ cup sour cream

Nutritional value per serving:

Calories: 630

Fats: 60g

Carbohydrates: 3g

Salt: 4.44g

Saturated fat: 10.8g

Fiber: 0.1g

Place half the lemon juice in a screw-topped jar with the olive oil and three tablespoons of the herbs. Season generously and shake well to combine, then store in the fridge for 2–3 days to allow the flavours to develop.

Preheat the broiler. Skin the salmon, then run your fingers against the grain of the flesh and remove the pin bones with tweezers. Place the coriander seeds on a baking sheet and toast under the grill for a few minutes. Allow to cool, then crush in a pestle and mortar until coarsely ground. Place the crushed coriander seeds in a bowl and add the salt, lemon rind and a good grinding of black pepper. Lay out a double layer of plastic wrap at least twice the size of the salmon and scatter over half the salt mixture and then sprinkle half of the remaining lemon juice on top. Cover with the salmon and scatter over the remaining salt mixture, finishing with the rest of the lemon juice. Wrap well with the plastic wrap, place on a baking sheet and chill for 24 hours.

Unwrap the salmon, then scrape off and discard the first marinade. Stir the remaining tablespoon of herbs into the mustard. Lay out a fresh piece of plastic wrap and smear the top of the salmon with half of the mustard mixture. Place the smeared side of the salmon down on the plastic wrap and smear the other side using the rest of the mustard mixture. Wrap tightly in the plastic wrap, place on a baking sheet and chill for another 24 hours.

Remove the salmon from the fridge and slice as thinly as possible. Arrange a few slices in the center of each serving plate. Remove the herb oil from the fridge and shake well to combine, then drizzle a little on to each plate. Dot the sour cream around the edges of the plates to serve.

hot-pickled mackerel

2 large or 4 small mackerel, cleaned and
   beheaded
salt
1 heaped tablespoon flour
2 tablespoons olive oil
$^1/_2$ onion, peeled and finely sliced
1 garlic clove, peeled and crushed
1 mild green chile, sliced
1 tablespoon chopped parsley
1 bay leaf, torn
6 peppercorns, roughly crushed
3-4 sprigs thyme
4 tablespoons sherry vinegar (or any other
   good vinegar)
2 tablespoons water

Chop each mackerel straight through the bone to give 4-6 thick steaks (your fish merchant will do this for you). Sprinkle with salt and dust with flour. Heat the oil in a shallow skillet and when it has a blue haze, put in the fish and fry gently until golden and firm (4-8 minutes depending on thickness). Transfer to a wide shallow dish.

Add the onion, garlic and sliced chile to the oil remaining in the pan (or a little new oil, if using leftovers) and fry gently for a few moments so that the flavors blend. Add the remaining ingredients and allow the mixture to bubble up. Pour this warm scented bath, unstrained, over the fish. Cover loosely with a clean cloth, and leave overnight, at least, in a cool place. Ready to eat in a day, better in two.

Nutritional value per serving:
Calories: 301
Fats: 22g
Carbohydrates: 7g
Salt: 0.42g
Saturated fat: 3.8g
Fibre: 0.6g

palm-heart salad with crab

1 can palmhearts, sliced into fine ribbons

6 tablespoons olive oil

2 tablespoons lime juice

shake of Tabasco sauce

1 teaspoon rough salt

To serve

1 Romaine lettuce, shredded

about 2¼ cups crab meat (save the
   carapace for serving)

shredded fresh coconut

Combine the palmhearts with the dressing ingredients, leave to marinate for an hour or two, toss with the lettuce and crab meat and finish with finely shredded coconut.

TIP

To prepare canned palmhearts (perfect for the dish), cut off any tough outside pieces and use a potato-peeler to cut tagliatelli-like ribbons – also a good technique should you manage to lay your hands on fresh palmhearts.

Nutritional value per serving:

Calories: 297

Fats: 23g

Carbohydrates: 3g

Salt: 2.22g

Saturated fat: 4.1g

Fiber: 1.6g

manhattan **clam** chowder

unscented vegetable oil

5 medium onions, peeled, cut into large dice

8 garlic cloves, finely chopped

1 head of celery, washed, peeled and diced

4 strips smoked bacon

10lb fresh clams, washed and rinsed of sand
  and grit

2$\frac{1}{2}$ cups dry white wine

2 quarts thick tomato juice

4 quarts fish broth

2 teaspoons Tabasco sauce

2 bay leaves

5 corn on the cob, cooked and kernels removed

9-10 medium potatoes, diced and cooked

12 plum tomatoes, peeled, pitted and diced

1 tablespoon superfine sugar

salt and freshly-ground black pepper

$\frac{1}{2}$ cup flat-leaf parsley, washed, dried and
  chopped, to garnish

Heat a little oil in a saucepan that is large enough to cook the clams. Add the onion, garlic, celery and bacon, then sauté until soft. Turn up the heat and add the clams and white wine. Cover with a lid and cook for about 4-5 minutes until the clams open. Remove the clams from the shells, discarding any that have not opened; reserve 12 for garnishing and set the rest aside.

Return the pan to the heat with the cooking liquid. Add the tomato juice, fish broth, Tabasco, and bay leaves and bring to a boil; simmer for 20 minutes. Season, then add the sweetcorn, potatoes, clams, tomatoes, and sugar. Check the seasoning, pour into a bowl, sprinkle with parsley and garnish with the clams in their shells.

Nutritional value per serving:

Calories: 174

Fats: 4g

Carbohydrates: 21g

Salt: 1.69g

Saturated fat: 0.8g

Fiber: 2.8g

scallops with gingerroot, scallions, & tamarind

1 tablespoon tamarind paste

$^3/_4$in piece of gingerroot, peeled and grated

2 scallions, thinly sliced lengthways and soaked
  in iced water

3 tablespoons vegetable oil, plus more for frying

1 tablespoon toasted sesame oil

12 scallops

salt

Place the tamarind paste in a saucepan with 4 tablespoons of water and heat gently, stirring to extract as much of the tamarind as possible. Set aside and allow to cool.

Strain and combine with the grated gingerroot, drained scallions and both types of oil.

Season the scallops with salt. Get a skillet good and hot and then oil it lightly. When the oil is hot, fry the scallops over as high a heat as you can manage for no more than 45 seconds on each side.

Place the scallops on small shallow plates or, better still, in well-scrubbed scallop shells, and spoon over the tamarind mixture.

TIP

If the scallops are really thick, they will sometimes remain cold and uncooked in the middle in the time it takes the exterior to cook perfectly. You can avoid this - and make the scallops go further - by cutting them across into two rounds.

Nutritional value per serving:

Calories: 214

Fats: 12g

Carbohydrates: 3g

Salt: 0.92g

Saturated fat: 1.7g

Fiber: 0.1g

cellophane noodle salad with chicken & shrimps

2½ cups Chinese mushrooms (wood ears)

2½ cups chicken broth

2 skinless chicken breasts

3 cups cellophane noodles

3oz mooli or French radishes

3 tablespoons *nam pla* (Thai fish sauce)

3 tablespoons lime juice, freshly squeezed

1 scant tablespoon superfine sugar

2-4 Thai red chiles, pitted and finely chopped

1 red onion, thinly sliced

2 scallions, thinly sliced at an angle

a few tender celery leaves (optional)

32 cooked large shrimp or 48 smaller shrimps

2 cups cilantro leaves

salt and freshly ground pepper

sprigs of cilantro and a couple of red and green
    chiles, to garnish

Put the mushrooms into a bowl, cover with warm water and allow to reconstitute for about 15 minutes. Drain, rinse and trim off any hard bits. Slice into thin strips.

Bring the chicken broth to a boil, add salt and slip in the chicken breasts; bring back to the boil and simmer gently for 8 minutes. Remove from the heat, cover and allow to cool. Then slice the chicken into thin pieces.

Put the noodles into another bowl, cover with boiling water and allow to stand for 5 minutes. Drain, cut into 3-4in lengths with a knife or clean scissors. Peel the mooli or radishes and slice very thinly. Put in a bowl of iced water to crisp up.

Mix the fish sauce, lime juice, sugar, and chopped chiles in a large bowl. Add the onions, scallions, celery leaves, and wood ears and mix well.

Drain the mooli well and add with the noodles, shrimps, chicken and cilantro to the other ingredients. Toss gently. Taste and correct seasoning. Serve garnished with cilantro sprigs and a few slices of red and green chiles.

Nutritional value per serving:

Calories: 206

Fats: 3g

Carbohydrates: 24g

Salt: 1.88g

Saturated fat: 0.4g

Fiber: 1g

steamed sea bass with black bean sauce

$^1/_2$in piece of gingerroot, peeled
   and thinly sliced
4 scallions, halved lengthways
1 sea bass, weighing about 1$^3/_4$lb
4 heads of pak choi, trimmed
3 tablespoons vegetable oil

Black bean sauce
3 tablespoons fermented black beans,
   roughly chopped
1 tablespoon soy sauce
1 dessertspoon medium dry sherry
1 dessertspoon rice vinegar
pepper

To serve
1 dessertspoon toasted sesame oil
1 dessertspoon sesame seeds, toasted in a
   dry skillet
1 tablespoon chopped cilantro leaves

Make the black bean sauce: combine the black beans, soy sauce, sherry, rice vinegar and a generous seasoning of pepper, together with 2 tablespoons of water. Set aside.

Place the gingerroot and scallions inside the fish's cavity. Arrange the stuffed fish and pak choi on a plate in a steamer and cook for 10-15 minutes, or until the fish is just cooked. Transfer the fish and pak choi to a low oven and keep warm. Pour the fish juices into the black bean sauce.

Heat a skillet and, when hot, add the oil. Seconds later, add the black bean sauce mixture and stir to emulsify, cooking the sauce for about 1 minute. Remove from the heat.

Remove the flesh from the carcass of the fish and serve it on top of the pak choi with a generous scoop of the sauce, a drizzle of sesame seed oil, a sprinkling of toasted sesame seeds and a little fresh cilantro.

Nutritional value per serving:
Calories: 265
Fats: 13g
Carbohydrates: 4g
Salt: 1.17g
Saturated fat: 1.7g
Fiber: 0.5g

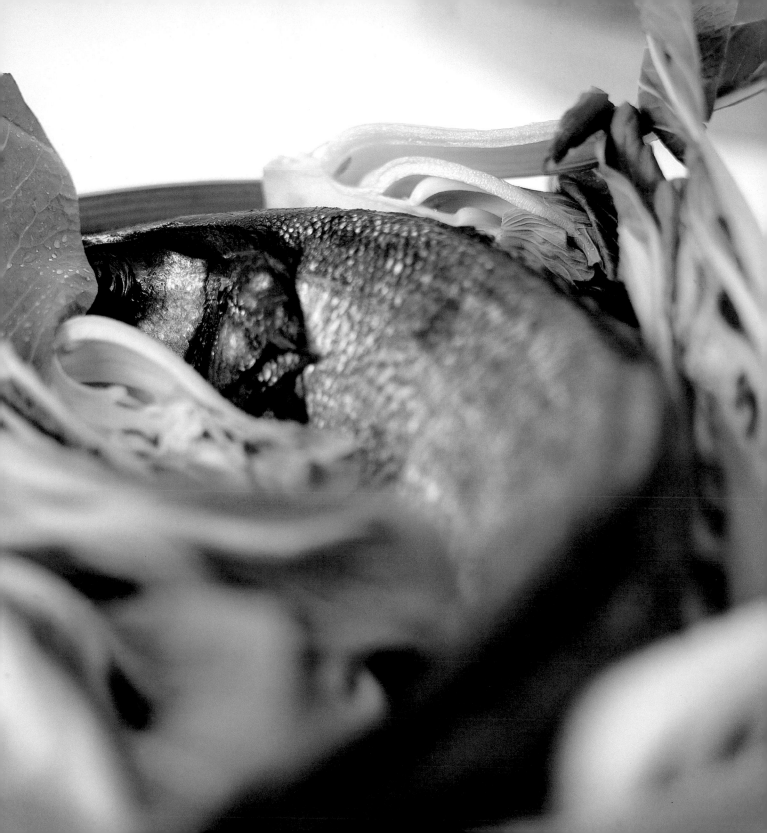

meatballs in broth with oregano

Meatballs

1 tablespoon rice

1$^1/_2$ cups (12oz) finely ground meat
    (pork and/or beef)

1 egg, mixed with a fork

1 garlic clove, very finely chopped

$^1/_2$ onion, very finely chopped

1 tablespoon chopped or crumbled oregano

$^1/_2$ teaspoon ground allspice

1 teaspoon finely chopped fresh chile or
    $^1/_2$ teaspoon chile flakes

salt

chopped tomato, to serve

Broth

5 cups strong chicken, beef or marrow-bone
    broth

1-2 habanero or malagueta chiles

1-2 sprigs dried oregano

Put the rice in a small bowl with enough boiling water to cover, and leave to soak and swell for about 20 minutes. Drain the rice and put it in the food processor with the rest of the meatball ingredients. Process all to a paste. With wet hands (keep a bowl of warm water handy for rinsing your fingers), form the mixture into about 24 bite-sized balls.

Bring the broth to a boil with the chile and oregano (tied into a scrap of cheesecloth for ease of removal). Slip in the meatballs and bring back to a simmer. Put the lid on loosely and leave to cook gently until the meatballs are tender – 20-25 minutes. Serve in bowls, finished with a little chopped tomato.

Nutritional value per serving:

Calories: 203

Fats: 10g

Carbohydrates: 7g

Salt: 1.44g

Saturated fat: 3.6g

Fiber: 0.5g

seared beef roll with gingerroot, carrot & bell peppers

1lb thinly sliced piece of steak, trimmed

8in piece fresh gingerroot, peeled and cut into thin matchsticks

2 large carrots, peeled and cut into thin matchsticks

6 jalapeño chiles, pitted and cut into thin matchsticks

2 red or yellow bell peppers, halved, pitted and cut into thin matchsticks

1 can of palm-hearts, drained and cut into thin matchsticks

a little olive oil

Place the steak on a piece of plastic wrap and cover with another piece. Batter with a rolling pin until you have achieved a rectangle that is 3in x 4in in total, trimming down any ragged pieces around the edges – these can be used in another dish or for a sauce. Remove and discard the plastic wrap.

Layer the gingerroot, carrots, jalapeño chiles, bell peppers, and hearts of palm matchsticks on to the middle of the beef, leaving two thirds of the meat uncovered with at least a $\frac{1}{2}$in border at the bottom edge. Roll up the beef around the vegetables, forming a tight tube similar to a sushi roll.

Heat a large skillet. Add a little olive oil and when the oil is smoking, add the steak roll to the pan and sear evenly on all sides. Using a pair of tongs, remove the beef roll from the pan and transfer to a chopping board. Cut in half and then into quarters. Arrange in warmed wide-rimmed bowls and serve with a small dish of teriyaki dipping sauce and some Thai sticky rice, if liked.

TIP

The steak needs to be a thin slice in one whole piece, otherwise you'll have great difficulty making the recipe work. Alternatively, try securing the roll with cocktail sticks which can be removed before carving.

Nutritional value per serving:

Calories: 264

Fats: 9g

Carbohydrates: 17g

Salt: 0.28g

Saturated fat: 2.5g

Fiber: 4.5g

delicious
dinners

french **onion** soup

½ stick butter

12 medium onions, thinly sliced

7½ cups good beef, chicken or vegetable broth

6 slices French bread (baguette), ½in thick,
   toasted

1 cup Gruyère cheese, grated

salt and freshly-ground pepper

Melt the butter in a saucepan. Add the onions and cook over a low heat for about 40-60 minutes with the lid off, stirring frequently – the onions should be dark and well caramelized but not burnt. Add the broth, season with salt and freshly-ground pepper, bring to a boil and cook for a further 10 minutes. Ladle into deep soup bowls, and put a piece of toasted baguette covered with grated cheese on top of each one. Pop under the grill until the cheese melts and turns golden. Serve immediately but beware – it will be very hot. Bon appetit!

Nutritional value per serving:

Calories: 280

Fats: 12g

Carbohydrates: 34g

Salt: 1.97g

Saturated fat: 7.3g

Fibre: 3.5g

cornmeal & potato soup

2-3 large potatoes, peeled and chunked

1 thick slice pumpkin, skinned and cut into
   chunks

5 cups chicken or beef broth or plain water

1 onion, finely chopped

2-3 garlic cloves, finely chopped

4 level tablespoons coarse-milled cornmeal

1 teaspoon chile flakes or finely chopped
   fresh chile

handful fresh basil leaves, stripped from
   the stalks

2 hard-boiled eggs, peeled and quartered

salt

Put the potatoes, pumpkin, and broth or water in a roomy pan with the onions and garlic. Bring to a boil, stir in the cornmeal, add a little salt and bring back to a boil. Put the lid on loosely, turn down the heat, and simmer for 30-40 minutes until the polenta is perfectly soft and the vegetables are tender. Finish with chile flakes, basil and quartered hard-boiled eggs.

Nutritional value per serving:

Calories: 204

Fats: 4g

Carbohydrates: 34g

Salt: 1.37g

Saturated fat: 0.9g

Fiber: 2.9g

jerusalem artichoke & mushroom stew

2lb Jerusalem artichokes

1 lemon

4 tablespoons olive oil

2 large onions, finely chopped

2 garlic cloves, finely chopped

3 cups mushrooms, diced

1 teaspoon dried thyme

1 small wine glass white wine

2 tablespoons green olives, pitted and chopped

1 slice stale bread, crumbled

1 hard-boiled egg, chopped

salt and freshly-ground black pepper

To serve

crumbled white cheese or hard-boiled egg

crisp lettuce leaves for scooping

Peel the artichokes carefully and divide into bite-sized pieces. As you peel each root, drop it into a bowl full of cold water into which you have squeezed a little lemon juice.

Heat the oil in a roomy casserole and fry the chopped onion and garlic until soft and golden (don't let it brown). Push aside and add the mushrooms. As soon as they yield up their juices, add the artichokes and the olives. Let them sizzle for a moment. Stir in the thyme, season with salt and pepper, pour in the wine and same volume of water, and let everything bubble up.

Turn down the heat, cover loosely, and leave to simmer very gently for an hour until the roots are perfectly tender. Stir in the crumbs - they'll soak up all the aromatic juices, leaving the tubers bathed in a deliciously fragrant dressing. Crumble over cheese or hard-boiled egg and serve with crisp lettuce leaves to scoop up the stew.

Nutritional value per serving:

Calories: 332

Fats: 14g

Carbohydrates: 42g

Salt: 0.72g

Saturated fat: 2.1g

Fiber: 5g

tagliatelle with **roasted chicken leg, mushrooms, & chile**

8 chicken legs (preferably free-range)

2 tablespoons olive oil

3½ cups (14oz) fresh tagliatelle

6 shallots, finely chopped

½ red chile, pitted and finely chopped

11oz shiitake mushrooms, sliced

4 tablespoons chopped fresh cilantro

Preheat the oven to 350°F. Place the chicken legs in a roasting pan and drizzle with a little olive oil. Season and roast for 20-30 minutes, depending on the size of the legs, until just tender and cooked through.

Increase the oven temperature to 400°F and roast the chicken legs for another 10 minutes or until the skin is crisp and golden brown.

Meanwhile, cook the tagliatelle in a large saucepan of boiling salted water for 2 minutes until *al dente*. Drain and quickly refresh under cold running water.

Heat the remaining tablespoon of olive oil in a large non-stick skillet and add the shallots. Cook for 1 minute, stirring, then add the chile and shiitake mushrooms. Increase the heat and cook for a further 2 minutes, stirring constantly.

Mix the tagliatelle into the mushroom mixture with most of the cilantro, reserving some for garnish. Season to taste. Divide the pasta between warmed wide-rimmed bowls and arrange two chicken legs on top of each serving. Garnish with the remaining cilantro and serve at once.

Nutritional value per serving:

Calories: 773

Fats: 38g

Carbohydrates: 56g

Salt: 0.69g

Saturated fat: 1.1g

Fiber: 2.9g

oven-baked **bream** with root vegetables

4 medium sweet potatoes, peeled and cut
   into chunks

4 medium potatoes, peeled and cut into chunks

4 medium smallish yellow onions, skinned and
   quartered

4 medium ripe firm tomatoes, cut into chunks

1 glass dry white wine

4 tablespoons olive oil

1 sea bream, weighing about 2lb when cleaned,
   head left on

rough salt

chile flakes

Arrange the vegetables in a roasting pan, pour in the wine, trickle with the oil, and finish with liberal dusting of salt and chile flakes. Cover with aluminum foil, shiny-side down. Bake for 20 minutes, until the vegetables are nearly tender. Carefully remove the foil. Place the fish on the bed of vegetables, sprinkle with salt and chile flakes, replace the aluminum foil and bake for another 10 minutes, until the fish is cooked right through. It's ready when it feels firm to your finger. Remove and leave on one side for another 10 minutes, so that the heat can penetrate right through to the bone.

Nutritional value per serving:

Calories: 510

Fats: 17g

Carbohydrates: 48g

Salt: 1.05g

Saturated fat: 2.8g

Fibre: 6.1g

cod with pine nuts & golden raisins

1½lb cod or firm white fish on the bone

2½ cups water

6 black peppercorns

1 large Spanish onion, peeled and finely sliced

3 tablespoons of olive oil

⅓ cup golden raisins

1 teaspoon saffron strands

¾ cup fruity white wine

½ cup pine nuts

sea salt

Cut the fish off the bone (reserve this for stock) and slice the flesh into large chunks about 2in square. Pour the measured water into a pan, add the tail bone, and with the peppercorns simmer actively for 20 minutes to make a light broth. Strain the broth and pour over the golden raisins. Leave to stand for 15 minutes then drain, reserving ¾ cup of the liquid. Place the saffron to steep in this liquid.

In a large heavy saucepan, heat the olive oil over a medium heat and add the onion. Fry for 10 minutes, stirring frequently, until golden.

Turn the heat up to medium high and add the fish pieces to the pan. Fry for 3-4 minutes, turning several times, until slightly golden. Now add the wine to the pan and allow to bubble fiercely for 1 minute. Add the saffron liquid, the golden raisins and pine nuts and a good pinch of salt. Bring to a boil then turn the heat to low and leave to simmer for 10 minutes. Check seasoning before serving.

Nutritional value per serving:

Calories: 378

Fats: 19g

Carbohydrates: 18g

Salt: 0.34g

Saturated fat: 2.6g

Fibre: 1.6g

fillet of turbot with cucumber spaghetti & herb sour cream

1 cup sour cream

juice of $1/2$ lemon

1 tablespoon chopped mixed herbs (such as dill, chervil and chives)

2 cucumbers

2 large carrots

2 tablespoons olive oil

4 x 5oz turbot fillets, unskinned

Place the sour cream in a bowl and add the lemon juice (reserving half a teaspoon) and the herbs. Season to taste and mix well, then cover with plastic wrap and place in the fridge to firm up. (This can be made the day before and left in the fridge overnight.)

Peel each cucumber, then cut in half and remove the seeds with a teaspoon; discard. Slice the cucumbers on a mandolin into long thin strips so that it resembles 'spaghetti' and place in a bowl. Peel the carrots and slice on the mandolin just like the cucumbers. Add to the cucumbers and gently mix to combine the colours. Add the reserved half a teaspoon of lemon juice, one teaspoon of the oil and season generously, mixing gently to combine. Cover with plastic wrap and set aside to allow the flavors to mingle.

Heat a non-stick skillet until very hot. Add the remaining olive oil to the pan and then add the fish fillets, skin-side down. Cook for 4-5 minutes, until the skin is crisp and golden, then turn over and cook for another minute until tender. Season to taste.

Arrange the cucumber spaghetti in wide-rimmed bowls and place a piece of turbot on top of each one. Quickly dip two tablespoons into boiling water and use to shape the herb sour cream into a quenelle – you will probably have some left-over that can be used for another dish. Place one on each piece of fish and serve immediately with cumin-roasted new potatoes, if liked.

Nutritional value per serving:

Calories: 397

Fats: 24g

Carbohydrates: 10g

Salt: 0.41g

Saturated fat: 11g

Fiber: 2.6g

rice with **squid** & mussels

2lb mussels, cleaned and scrubbed (discarding
  any open ones that don't close
  on being tapped)

4 tablespoons olive oil

1³/₄lb squid, cleaned and cut into tablespoon-
  sized pieces

2 garlic cloves, finely chopped

2¹/₃ cups Valencia rice (or a risotto rice)

1 x 14oz can chopped tomatoes

4 cups hot chicken broth

pinch of saffron threads, dissolved in a little
  hot water

1 tablespoon chopped parsley

3-4 lemons, halved

salt and freshly-ground black pepper

Put the mussels in a saucepan, cover with a lid and place over a moderate heat, shaking well. The mussels take 4 to 5 minutes to open. Remove the lid and set aside to cool.

Heat the olive oil in a flameproof casserole. Season the squid with salt and sauté for 5 minutes. Stir in the garlic and rice and sauté for 2 minutes. Add the tomatoes with their liquid and the broth. Bring to a boil, stir once and simmer for 20 minutes.

Meanwhile, remove the mussels from their shells, leaving a dozen or so intact for decoration. (Any mussels that have not opened should be discarded.) Strain the liquor from the saucepan, taking care to leave any grit behind. A couple of minutes before the end of rice cooking time, stir in the strained liquor and the mussels along with the saffron and its soaking liquid. Adjust the seasoning, stir in the parsley and serve with a lemon half.

How to debeard mussels

To remove the beards from mussels, hold the mussel with the pointed end away from you. Pull downwards on the beard to remove it. Scrub the mussels well before cooking.

Nutritional value per serving:

Calories: 457

Fats: 11g

Carbohydrates: 59g

Salt: 1.69g

Saturated fat: 1.3g

Fiber: 1.8g

shrimp & feta risotto

5 cups vegetable broth

1/2 cup small peeled cooked shrimp

1 red chile, pitted and finely chopped

4 tablespoons olive oil

1 x 9oz can tomatoes, drained

good pinch of dried oregano

1/2 stick butter

1 onion, finely chopped

4 whole celery stalks, finely chopped

2 carrots, finely chopped

3 garlic cloves, finely chopped

1 1/2 cups Arborio rice (risotto rice)

1/2 bottle of good white wine

2/3 cup feta cheese

salt and freshly-ground black pepper

Arugula & cucumber salad

1 1/2 cups arugula leaves

1 cucumber, chopped

2 tablespoons olive oil

juice of 1 lemon

Put the vegetable broth in a saucepan and bring to a boil. While the broth is heating, sauté the shrimp and finely chopped chile in 3 tablespoons of the olive oil until golden, then pull off the heat. Purée the canned tomatoes with a little oregano and the remaining olive oil, and place to one side.

Gently melt the butter in a large flameproof casserole and add the onion, celery, carrots, and garlic. Sweat gently for 10 minutes until softened. Now add the Arborio rice and stir for 3 minutes. Pour in the white wine and cook, stirring from time to time, until the rice mixture becomes firm.

Slowly start to add the simmering vegetable broth to the rice, 2/3 cup at a time every 2-3 minutes, stirring occasionally. Once all the broth has been added, gently stir in the puréed tomatoes, then crumble in the feta cheese. Add the parsley followed by the cooked shrimp. Season to taste with salt and pepper.

Make the salad by tossing the arugula leaves and cucumber with the oil, lemon juice, and seasoning to taste. Serve the risotto with the salad.

Nutritional value per serving:

Calories: 654

Fats: 33g

Carbohydrates: 61g

Salt: 3.24g

Saturated fat: 12.2g

Fiber: 4.7g

roast chump of **lamb** with garlic

8-10 new potatoes, scrubbed and cut
   into ½in slices

4 tablespoons olive oil

6 garlic cloves, finely chopped

2 teaspoons fresh thyme leaves

4 x 6oz pieces of lamb loin

2 zucchini, cut into rough triangles

4 ripe, firm tomatoes, quartered

Preheat the oven to 350°F. Place the potatoes in a large roasting pan with two tablespoons of the olive oil and season generously. Toss to coat and roast for 20 minutes, then add the garlic and thyme, tossing again to coat and roast for another 8-10 minutes or until the potatoes are crisp and tender. Leave the garlic and thyme juices in the roasting pan.

Meanwhile, heat a heavy-based roasting pan on the hob. Season the lamb chops.

Add the remaining two tablespoons of olive oil to the pan and then add the lamb pieces. Sear on each side for a minute or so until well sealed and golden brown in patches. Place each piece skin-side down and roast for 10-12 minutes until just tender but still slightly pink in the middle. Transfer to a warmed dish and leave to rest in a warm place.

Add the zucchini to the same roasting pan with the remaining garlic and thyme, tossing to coat in the juices and roast for 5 minutes. Add the tomatoes, tossing again to coat, and cook for another 5 minutes, remembering to turn the vegetables occasionally.

Meanwhile, arrange the potatoes on warmed serving plates and spoon over the cooked vegetables. Carve the lamb and arrange on top, then drizzle all of the meat and vegetable juices on top as a sauce. Serve immediately.

Nutritional value per serving:

Calories: 615

Fats: 41g

Carbohydrates: 31g

Salt: 0.27g

Saturated fat: 16.5g

Fiber: 3.7g

lamb & apricot tagine

²/₃ cup dried apricots

1lb shoulder of lamb, off the bone, trimmed of
  fat and cut into chunks

1 teaspoon powdered ginger

1 teaspoon ground cinnamon

2 teaspoon freshly-ground black pepper

pinch of mace or nutmeg

1 large onion, peeled and grated

½ stick unsalted butter, cut into small pieces

1 small bunch fresh cilantro

1 small bunch fresh flat-leaf parsley

sea salt

Pour sufficient boiling water over the apricots to just cover them and leave to soak.
Place the meat in a large heavy casserole or better still, a tagine if you have one.
Sprinkle over the spices, the grated onion, and the butter. Place the casserole over a
low heat and cook for 5 minutes, stirring regularly, until the butter melts and the spices
give off their scent – the meat should not brown. Tie the herbs together in a bunch and
add them to the pot. Pour in just enough water to barely cover the meat. Bring to a boil
then turn down the heat and leave to simmer gently for 1 hour.

Now add the apricots to the tagine, together with their liquid, and salt to taste. Cook
for a further 30 minutes, until the apricots are plumped up. Taste to check the
seasoning, remove the bunches of herbs and serve with flat bread.

How to make herb bouquet

Gather the herb stalks together and tie tightly with kitchen string. Secure the
ends tightly.

Nutritional value per serving:

Calories: 346

Fats: 19g

Carbohydrates: 19g

Salt: 0.5g

Saturated fat: 10.5g

Fiber: 2.9g

shoulder of lamb with yogurt & cardamom

4lb shoulder of lamb, boned and rolled

4 garlic cloves, cut into slivers

4 tablespoons cardamom pods

3 tablespoons olive oil

juice and grated rind of 1 lemon

¼ teaspoon saffron strands

⅔ cup Greek yogurt

2 tablespoons brown sugar

salt and freshly-ground black pepper

Season the lamb with salt and pepper and make deep cuts in it with a sharp knife. Insert the garlic slivers into the cuts. Crush the cardamom pods then sprinkle over the cardamom seeds and rub them in. Leave at room temperature for 5 hours (or overnight in the fridge). Preheat the oven to 400°F. Heat the oil in a roasting pan, add the lamb and brown all over. Transfer to the oven and roast for 20-30 minutes, until well colored. Remove from the oven and leave to cool slightly while you prepare the lemon yogurt coating. Reduce the oven to 325°F. Put the lemon juice and saffron in a small pan and heat gently. Leave to cool, then mix with the lemon rind, yogurt, and sugar. Pour half this mixture over the lamb. Return the lamb to the oven and cook, adding more lemon yogurt every 30 minutes or so, for about 2½-3 hours, until the lamb is very tender and is topped with a golden yogurt crust. Allow to cool slightly before serving.

How to grind cardamom pods

Grinding cardamom pods in a pestle and mortar releases the small black seeds from inside the pods.

Nutritional value per serving:

Calories: 620

Fats: 46g

Carbohydrates: 8g

Salt: 0.56g

Saturated fat: 21.4g

Fiber: 0.1g

braised rabbit with bacon, tomato, & beans

1 young rabbit (about 3½ lb), jointed

2 tablespoons all-purpose flour

2 tablespoons olive oil

2 tablespoons unsalted butter

3 smoked bacon strips

⅔ cup dry white wine

1½ cups well-flavored meat broth

3oz sun-blushed tomatoes

2oz shelled fresh beans, cooked

salt and freshly-ground black pepper

Marinade

12 garlic cloves, peeled but left whole

1 small bay leaf

6 rosemary sprigs, plus extra to garnish

2 tablespoons olive oil

Put the rabbit joints in a dish with all the marinade ingredients. Cover and leave to marinate for 24 hours.

Preheat the oven to 300°F. Remove the rabbit from the marinade and dry well, then coat it in the flour. Heat the olive oil and the butter in a large casserole until very hot, then season the rabbit joints and brown them in the hot fat. Add the garlic cloves from the marinade and the smoked bacon and cook for 3-4 minutes. Drain off any excess fat, then return to the heat, pour in the white wine and tuck in the rosemary sprigs and bay leaf from the marinade. Pour over the meat broth and bring to a boil. Reduce the heat, cover and place in the oven. Cook for 1 hour, then add the sun-blushed tomatoes and cook for 15 minutes longer.

Remove from the oven and strain off the liquid into a saucepan. Simmer until it is thick enough to coat the back of a spoon, then stir in the beans and season to taste. Pour the sauce over the rabbit, garnish with a little rosemary and serve. Creamy mashed potato, lightened with olive oil, makes a good accompaniment.

Nutritional value per serving:

Calories: 593

Fats: 32g

Carbohydrates: 12g

Salt: 2.12g

Saturated fat: 11.7g

Fiber: 0.8g

persian **beef** stew

2/3 cup yellow split peas

1 tablespoon extra-virgin olive oil

1 large onion, finely chopped

12oz lean braising beef, trimmed of fat
   and cubed

1 teaspoon ground cinnamon

¼ teaspoon grated nutmeg

2½ cups beef stock

1 large cooking apple, peeled, cored and
   thickly sliced

1 sweet potato, peeled and cubed

juice of 1 lemon

2 tablespoons runny honey

½ cup raisins

1 cup frozen peas

salt and freshly-ground black pepper

Put the split peas in a bowl, cover with water, and leave for 1 hour.

Heat the oil in a large, deep skillet, add the onion and soften gently for 3 minutes. Add the meat and continue cooking, stirring continuously, until the meat is sealed and the onion becomes slightly golden. Stir in the cinnamon and nutmeg, add the broth and simmer, covered, for 30 minutes.

Drain and rinse the split peas. Put into a saucepan of boiling water and boil for 5 minutes. Drain. Add the split peas to the skillet with the apple and potato. Bring back to a boil, cover and simmer for 15 minutes.

Add the lemon juice, honey, raisins, and green peas, pushing the raisins and the peas into the pan without breaking up the apple. Continue to simmer for 15-20 minutes. Season with salt and pepper if necessary, and serve.

Nutritional value per serving:

Calories: 405

Fats: 9g

Carbohydrates: 55g

Salt: 0.99g

Saturated fat: 2.7g

Fiber: 5.8g

calf's liver & bacon
with puy lentils

4 tablespoons olive oil

7oz smoked bacon, cut into strips

2 cloves garlic, crushed

20 baby onions

$1/2$ cup Puy lentils, soaked for 24 hours

$2 1/2$ cups chicken broth

13oz calf's liver, sliced

4 tablespoons balsamic vinegar

4 tablespoons chopped parsley

salt and freshly-ground black pepper

Pour half the oil into a large sauté pan and sauté the smoked bacon, garlic, and onions until golden brown. Add the soaked lentils and add to the pan with the chicken broth. Leave to simmer for $1 1/2$-2 hours.

Towards the end of the cooking time, pour the rest of the oil into a second large sauté pan over a moderately high heat. Season the liver and seal in the hot oil on both sides, then transfer to the pan containing the lentils.

Cook the liver with the lentils for another 10 minutes. Mix in the balsamic vinegar and serve sprinkled with chopped parsley.

Nutritional value per serving:

Calories: 410

Fats: 23g

Carbohydrates: 16g

Salt: 2.9g

Saturated fat: 5.8g

Fiber: 3.3g

layered fajitas

Fajitas

1^1/$_2$ cups plain flour

good pinch of salt

corn oil, for frying

Filling

2 x 14oz tins of red beans (or 1 cup dried beans
soaked for 24 hours)

2 tablespoons corn oil

1 onion, chopped

1 red chile, pitted and chopped

1 garlic clove, chopped

^{1}/$_2$ bunch of fresh cilantro, chopped

dash of Tabasco sauce

juice of 1 lime

^{1}/$_2$ cup sour cream

Salsa

4 tomatoes, pitted and chopped

^{1}/$_2$ bunch of fresh cilantro (stalks and all),
chopped

^{1}/$_2$ red onion, chopped

3 tablespoons corn oil

Nutritional value per serving:

Calories: 530

Fats: 22g

Carbohydrates: 65g

Salt: 1.6g

Saturated fat: 5.9g

Fiber: 10.8g

First make the fajitas: pour the flour and salt into a mixing bowl, make a well in the center and add 1^1/$_4$ cups water. Mix together, adding a little more water, if necessary, until you have a firm dough. Knead the dough until nice and smooth, then cut into 6 pieces and shape into balls. Roll each ball out to a 7in round. Heat a non-stick skillet and dry-fry each fajita on both sides until it puffs up and immediately remove from the heat.

Make the filling: if using soaked dried beans, drain them, add to a saucepan of boiling water and cook gently for 2 hours; if using tinned beans, drain and add to a saucepan with 1^1/$_4$ cups water and cook gently for 30 minutes.

Add the corn oil to a saucepan and cook the onion, chile and garlic until softened. Add the drained beans and cook for a further 10 minutes, stirring, then start to mash the beans roughly with the back of a fork, adding the chopped cilantro, a dash of Tabasco and the lime juice. Stir well and pull from heat.

Make the salsa by mixing together all the ingredients.

Lay each fajita on a plate, spoon over a quarter of the bean filling, add a dollop of sour cream, drizzle with a little salsa and repeat layering your 5 fajitas until you come to the final fajita which you use as a lid, pressing down firmly. Top with the remaining salsa, place in the fridge and allow to set. Cut into pie wedges and eat outdoors.

TIP

If you like, you can add a pitted and chopped red chile to the salsa for some authentic chili heat.

fresh bean cassoulet with garlic cornmeal wedges

1³/₄ cups water or vegetable broth

²/₃ cup cornmeal

1 clove garlic, crushed

¹/₂ teaspoon dried mixed herbs

1 dessertspoon extra-virgin olive oil

1 onion, finely chopped

1 clove garlic, crushed

1 carrot, sliced

1oz fennel, roughly chopped

1 cup mushrooms, sliced

3 sprigs rosemary

1 bay leaf and 1 sprig thyme

1 x 14oz can cannellini beans, drained

4oz shelled fresh beans

4oz green beans, sliced diagonally

1¹/₄ cups vegetable broth

1 dessertspoon soy sauce

1 teaspoon cornflour, mixed with a little water

sea salt and freshly-ground black pepper

Nutritional value per serving:

Calories: 459

Fats: 9g

Carbohydrates: 77g

Salt: 2.93g

Saturated fat: 1g

Fiber: 15.1g

Bring the broth to a boil in a large saucepan. Add the cornmeal to the broth slowly, stirring continuously. When the mixture starts to thicken, add the garlic and mixed herbs and season. Continue to stir until the mixture resembles a smooth porridge, 4-5 minutes. Turn the cornmeal into a round, non-stick cake pan, smooth the surface and set aside to cool.

Sweat the onion and garlic with the olive oil in a covered skillet for 3-4 minutes. Add the carrot, fennel, mushrooms, and herbs to the pan and sweat for another 6-7 minutes. Add the beans and broth to the pan and bring to a boil. Simmer for 15-20 minutes. When the beans are tender, add the soy sauce and cornflour mixture to the pan and simmer for about 5 minutes more to thicken the sauce. Season. Grill the cornmeal wedges until crisp and brown and serve hot with the cassoulet.

How to cook and grill cornmeal

Pour cooked cornmeal into a greased round pan. Leave until cold then cut into triangles. Heat a ridged broiler pan, oil each piece of cornmeal and fry until charbroiled.

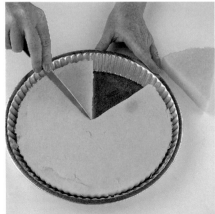

vegetable bake

6 tablespoons olive oil

3 sweet Spanish onions, diced

2 garlic cloves, finely chopped

3 large sprigs fresh oregano, roughly chopped.

2 smallish eggplants, cut into ¼in slices

5 zucchini, peeled if necessary and cut
   into ¼in slices

6 tomatoes, cut into ¼in slices

1lb fresh, young mozzarella cheese, cut
   into ¼in slices

5 tablespoons freshly grated Parmesan

6 sprigs dill

freshly-ground black pepper

Preheat the oven to 400°F.

Heat the oil in a skillet, add the onions and cook gently for 5 minutes to soften. Add the garlic and continue cooking for 3 minutes. Stir the oregano into the onion mixture and remove from the heat.

Put the eggplant slices on a baking pan in a single layer, sprinkle with salt and bake for 8 minutes until softened.

Put the onion and herb mixture into an ovenproof dish. Arrange the eggplant, zucchini, tomato, and mozzarella alternately in the dish, standing them on their sides. When they're all arranged, push down gently with the palms of your hands and season with black pepper. Place the dish in the oven and bake for about 1 hour. Sprinkle the Parmesan on top and bake for another 10 minutes.

Serve with the whole sprigs of dill scattered on top.

TIP

Fresh oregano is widely available. Dried won't be as good for aroma or flavor, but if you have to use it, add 1 tablespoon.

Nutritional value per serving:

Calories: 667

Fats: 46g

Carbohydrates: 25g

Salt: 2.14g

Saturated fat: 20.4g

Fiber: 7.8g

bean, pumpkin, & sweetcorn casserole

1 cup fresh, shelled beans

1lb piece pumpkin, skinned and chunked

1 tablespoon soft pork lard or oil

1 link soft chorizo, crumbled (or 4 slices bacon, diced)

2 large mild onions, finely chopped

1 red bell pepper, pitted and diced

1 carrot, scraped and coarsely grated

2½ cups fresh corn kernels

handful fresh basil leaves, chopped

salt

To finish

2 garlic cloves, skinned and roughly chopped

1 tablespoon paprika

pinch of powdered chili

1-2 tablespoons oil

salt

Put the shelled beans and the pumpkin in a roomy saucepan, add enough hot water to cover to a depth of two fingers, bring to a boil, reduce the heat, put the lid on and simmer until the pumpkin has melted to a soupy sauce and the beans are perfectly tender: 40-60 minutes.

Meanwhile, heat the lard or oil gently in a small skillet and fry the chorizo or diced bacon until it takes a little color. Add the onion, red bell pepper, and carrot, salt lightly and fry until soft and a little caramelised. Stir into the beans and simmer for another 10 minutes.

Meanwhile, put the corn kernels in the blender with a ladleful of the bean liquor and the basil leaves (reserve a few of the best). Process to a purée, stir into the beans and simmer for another 15 minutes – dilute with a little boiling water if it looks too thick.

To make the finishing oil, crush the garlic cloves with a little salt and work in the oil and spices. Serve in deep earthenware bowls, with a swirl of scarlet oil and a basil leaf to finish.

Nutritional value per serving:

Calories: 416

Fats: 17g

Carbohydrates: 50g

Salt: 0.9g

Saturated fat: 4.7g

Fiber: 12.5g

spinach greens with peanuts

l$\frac{1}{2}$lb spinach greens or other leaves

$\frac{1}{2}$ teaspoon salt

8 medium tomatoes, finely chopped

6-8 scallions, finely chopped

4 tablespoons pounded roasted peanuts

Cook the spinach in a tightly lidded saucepan in the water which clings to the leaves after washing. Sprinkle with salt to encourage the juices to run.

As soon as the leaves collapse and soften, remove the lid and add a layer of chopped tomatoes and chopped scallion. Sprinkle with the powdered peanuts, but do not stir. Turn down the heat, put the lid on loosely and simmer for about 15 minutes, until the tomato flesh has softened. Stir, put the lid on loosely again and simmer for another 15 minutes. Remove the lid and bubble up to evaporate any excess juices. Reverse the contents of the pan onto the serving dish, and finish with a sprinkle of whole roast peanuts.

TIP

A Brazilian dish of African origin, this dish can be made with a wide variety of edible greens including spinach of the tough evergreen variety, the young leaves of pumpkin, cassava and sweet potato, chard, and young cabbage. Serve as a vegetarian dish with soft cornmeal or rice.

Nutritional value per serving:

Calories: 138

Fats: 8g

Carbohydrates: 7g

Salt: 1.4g

Saturated fat: 1.5g

Fiber: 5.7g

lima beans with pumpkin

1 cup limas, soaked overnight

4 medium yellow-fleshed potatoes, peeled and
   cubed in bite-sized pieces

1lb pumpkin or any winter squash, cubed in
   bite-size pieces

2½ cups fresh or frozen sweetcorn

salt

chopped parsley, to serve

crumbled white cheese such as feta, to serve

Flavoring salsa

3 yellow chiles, pitted and chopped

1 small yellow onion, finely chopped

6 scallions, finely chopped with their green

3 garlic cloves, finely chopped

2 tablespoons olive oil

Cook the beans in a roomy saucepan with enough water to cover. Don't put the lid on. The water should tremble but never come off a boil. Allow 2 hours (1 hour if the beans are fresh) and cook until soft but not mushy. Add boiling water as and when necessary, but no salt.

Meanwhile, bubble up the salsa ingredients in a small saucepan, and set aside to combine the flavors.

When the beans are tender, add the vegetables and extra boiling water, salt, and the prepared salsa, and cook for another half hour, until the vegetables are perfectly soft. The dish should be moist but not soupy. Finish with a handful of chopped parsley and crumbled white cheese – feta is the right texture.

Nutritional value per serving:

Calories: 478

Fats: 12g

Carbohydrates: 76g

Salt: 0.79g

Saturated fat: 2.9g

Fiber: 14.2g

charbroiled **cornmeal** with roasted red & yellow peppers

2 quarts water

2 teaspoons salt

$1^1/_2$ cups coarse cornmeal

6 tablespoons olive tapenade

3 red bell peppers

3 yellow peppers

sea salt and freshly-ground pepper

Put the water into a deep saucepan and bring to a boil, add salt, then sprinkle the cornmeal in slowly, whisking all the time (this should take 3-4 minutes). Bring to a boil and when it starts to 'erupt like a volcano' turn the heat down to the absolute minimum and cook for about 40 minutes, stirring regularly. The cornmeal is cooked when it is very thick but not solid and comes away from the sides of the pan as you stir. As soon as the cornmeal is cooked, season with lots of pepper. Taste and add a little more sea salt if necessary. Pour the cooked cornmeal into a wet dish (use a lasagne dish: (9 x 7 x 2in) which is just perfect for this quantity, but you could use a Swiss roll pan and cut it into squares or diamonds when it is cold). Allow to get completely cold.

Preheat the oven to 475°F. Put the bell peppers on a baking sheet and bake for 20-30 minutes until the skin blisters and the flesh is soft. Put them into a bowl and cover tightly with plastic wrap for a few minutes; this will make them much easier to peel. Pull the skin off the bell peppers, remove the stalks and pits. Do not wash or you will lose the precious sweet juices. Divide each into 2 or 3 pieces along the natural division.

To serve: cut the cornmeal into slices $^1/_2$-$^3/_4$in thick and chargrill, pan-broil or fry. Put it directly on to the bars of the broiler on the highest heat without oil and cook until it is hot through and grill-marked on each side. Spread a spoonful of tapenade on to each slice and top with the roasted red and yellow bell peppers.

Nutritional value per serving:

Calories: 249

Fats: 9g

Carbohydrates: 36g

Salt: 2.24g

Saturated fat: 0.9g

Fiber: 1.5g

outdoor
food

salt-griddled shrimp with lime & garlic

20 extra-large uncooked shrimp, shell on
4 tablespoons virgin olive oil
juice of $1/4$ lemon
$1/2$ teaspoon chopped thyme
$1/2$ teaspoon chopped oregano
2 tablespoons coarse salt
$1/4$ teaspoon garlic salt
freshly-ground black pepper

Lime and garlic sauce
$3/4$ cup fish broth
juice of 3 limes
grated rind of 1 lime
1 garlic clove, crushed
1 small red onion, finely chopped
2 tablespoons chopped flat-leaf parsley
2 tablespoons chilled unsalted butter, diced

Cut down the back of each shrimp shell with a sharp knife or kitchen scissors and lift out the black intestinal vein, leaving the shell on. Coat the shrimp in the olive oil and lemon juice and season with black pepper. In a bowl, mix together the herbs and salts. Dredge the shrimp in the mixture, ensuring they are well coated. Grill the salt-crusted shrimp on a hot barbecue or a ridged broil pan for 3-4 minutes on each side.

Meanwhile, make the sauce. Put all the ingredients except the butter in a pan and bring to a boil. Remove from the heat and whisk in the butter.

Remove the shrimp from the barbecue and arrange on a serving dish. Pour the sauce around them and serve.

Nutritional value per serving:
Calories: 253
Fats: 17g
Carbohydrates: 2g
Salt: 4.52g
Saturated fat: 4.8g
Fiber: 0.4g

squid ink pasta with shrimp salad

30 fresh medium shrimp, peeled

olive oil

1lb 2oz fresh squid ink tagliatelle

30 asparagus spears, peeled and blanched

1 bunch of scallions, washed, roots trimmed,
    finely sliced

10 plum tomatoes, skinned, pitted and diced

2 red chiles, pitted and finely sliced

1/2 cup snipped chives

salt and freshly-ground black pepper

Dressing

3 tablespoons white wine vinegar

1 tablespoon superfine sugar

5 tablespoons extra-virgin olive oil

First make the dressing: blend the vinegar and sugar in a blender or food processor for 20 seconds. Add the oil slowly in a steady stream until emulsified.

Preheat the barbecue or broiler. Brush the shrimp with olive oil, season, place on the barbecue, and cook evenly on all sides. Bring a saucepan of salted water with a little olive oil to a boil, cook the pasta al dente, drain, and refresh.

Place the shrimp, pasta, and asparagus in a large bowl and pour over the dressing. Add the scallions, tomatoes, chiles, and chives; toss well. Season and serve.

Nutritional value per serving:

Calories: 244

Fats: 8g

Carbohydrates: 31g

Salt: 0.45g

Saturated fat: 1g

Fiber: 2.5g

dressed sardines

12 fresh (as fresh as possible) sardines

2 tablespoons plain flour

a little olive oil, for coating

Dressing

large bunch of mint, finely shredded

2 tablespoons red wine vinegar

pinch of celery salt

2 shallots, finely chopped

grated rind of 2 lemons

pinch of dried chili

2 tablespoons olive oil

salt and freshly-ground black pepper

First prepare the dressing: in a bowl, mix the mint, vinegar, celery salt, chopped shallots, lemon rind and chili. Place to one side.

Run a sharp knife along the underside (belly) of the sardine. Under very gentle running water, using the best kitchen tool of all, the index finger, remove the fish's innards. At this point, still under running water, gently scrape off any outer scales from the fish, ensuring you remove all of them – they come away easily using your thumb or a table knife. Using a dish towel, dry the sardines well to help avoid their sticking to the barbecue.

Pour the flour on to one large plate and drizzle a little olive oil on another. Dip the sardines into the flour on both sides to coat, and then lightly pull the fish through the olive oil. Place on the preheated hot barbecue and cook them for about 5 minutes on each side.

Finish the dressing by adding the oil and seasoning with salt and pepper. Lay the cooked sardines on a large plate and spoon over the delicious fresh, tangy dressing – the perfect accompaniment for sardines.

Nutritional value per serving:

Calories: 422

Fats: 25g

Carbohydrates: 7g

Salt: 1.13g

Saturated fat: 4.7g

Fiber: 0.3g

charbroiled **tuna** with green papaya salad

1lb 7oz small tuna fillet, trimmed

2 tablespoons tamarind paste

2 tablespoons brown sugar

2 red chiles, pitted and finely chopped

1 tablespoon *nam pla* (Thai fish sauce)

oil for grilling

salt and freshly-ground black pepper

1 lime, cut into wedges, to garnish

Green papaya salad

1 garlic clove, chopped

2 red chiles, pitted and chopped

1 teaspoon brown sugar

2 green papayas, peeled, pitted and shredded

juice of 2 limes

2 tablespoons *nam pla* (Thai fish sauce)

3/4 cup French beans, cooked

2 tablespoons roasted peanuts

10 red cherry tomatoes, halved

10 yellow cherry tomatoes, halved

Nutritional value per serving:

Calories: 398

Fats: 12g

Carbohydrates: 32g

Salt: 2.59g

Saturated fat: 3.2g

Fiber: 4.9g

Cut the tuna into 4 steaks across the fillet. In a bowl, combine the tamarind with the sugar, chiles, fish sauce, and some salt and pepper. Pour this mixture over the tuna and set aside for 1 hour to allow the flavors to meld.

For the salad, roughly crush the garlic, chiles, sugar, and a quarter of the shredded papaya in a mortar. Transfer to a bowl, add the lime juice and fish sauce and stir well. Add all the remaining ingredients, including the rest of the papaya, toss well and season to taste. Barbecue the tuna steaks or panbroil them as shown below. Remove from the heat and cut each steak into 4 slices. Arrange a pile of salad on each serving plate, top with the seared tuna, then garnish with the lime wedges and serve.

How to charbroil tuna steaks

Heat a ridged broil pan until very hot. Brush the tuna steaks with a little oil and season with salt and pepper. Charbroil for 2 minutes on each side, keeping them rare.

PREPARATION TIME: 20 MINUTES

COOKING TIME: 20 MINUTES

spiedinos of scallops, cod & pancetta

1 ciabatta loaf, cut into 12 cubes

4 tablespoons extra-virgin olive oil

12 slices of pancetta or smoked back bacon

12 shelled scallops, preferably with their corals

2lb cod or other firm white fish, cut into
   12 cubes

juice of 1-2 lemon(s), to serve

salt and freshly-ground black pepper

6 stout fennel sticks or long skewers
   (about 10in long)

Put the ciabatta chunks in a large mixing bowl, pour over the olive oil, and stir around well. Remove each chunk of bread and wrap a strip of pancetta around it. Then taking a skewer, first spear one piece of wrapped bread (skewering the pancetta on the wrapped side to ensure it doesn't fall off during cooking), then spear a scallop through the coral and then the white meat lengthways, then skewer a chunk of fish. Repeat this until you have 6 pieces, two of each ingredient on each skewer.

Lightly season the spiedinos, place on the hottest part of the barbecue and broil for 10 minutes on each side. Serve on a large plate with a squeeze of lemon juice.

How to prepare scallops

With the flat side of the scallop upwards, slide a sharp knife between the two halves of the shell to cut the nerve holding them closed. Remove and discard the top shell. Slide the knife underneath the exposed scallop and ease it off the shell. Discard the black tissue around it and cut off the black vein that runs around the side of the scallop.

Nutritional value per serving:

Calories: 406

Fats: 18g

Carbohydrates: 20g

Salt: 2.5g

Saturated fat: 4.7g

Fiber: 1.1g

broiled spiced spring **chicken**

2 small spring chickens or poussins, split open

4 tablespoons olive oil

juice of 1 lemon

1 teaspoon paprika

3 teaspoons coarse sea salt

1 teaspoon ground cumin

1 teaspoon cayenne pepper

2 tablespoons finely chopped fresh flat-leaf
   parsley

toasted cumin seeds

Mix together all the marinade ingredients and pour over the chickens. Leave for at least 2 hours.

Meanwhile, get the barbecue coals glowing and heat a ridged broiler pan, or heat the broiler to maximum. Broil the chickens for 25-30 minutes, placing them skin side down on the barbecue or broiler pan and skin side up under the broiler. Turn the chickens to expose the underside to the heat after 10 minutes and turn back after another 10 minutes so that you finish skin side to the heat source. Baste regularly with the marinade. Serve with quartered lemons and bowls of coarse sea salt and toasted cumin seeds.

Nutritional value per serving:

Calories: 797

Fats: 56g

Carbohydrates: 1g

Salt: 2.42g

Saturated fat: 0.4g

Fiber: 0.1g

broiled chicken with sweet chili sauce

Marinade

2 tablespoons sesame oil

2 garlic cloves, finely chopped

1 teaspoon finely chopped cilantro root

2 small fresh red chiles, finely chopped

2 tablespoons *nam pla* (Thai fish sauce)

1 teaspoon granulated sugar

4 boneless chicken breasts, with skin,
   cut into chunks

Hot and sweet sauce

6 tablespoons rice or white wine vinegar

4 tablespoons granulated sugar

$1/2$ teaspoon salt

2 garlic cloves, finely chopped

3 small fresh red chiles, finely chopped

In a large bowl, mix together all the ingredients for the marinade and leave to marinate for 30 minutes.

Meanwhile, make the hot and sweet sauce. In a small saucepan, heat the vinegar and sugar and stir until dissolved. Add the salt and simmer, stirring, until the liquid thickens. Remove from the heat, pour into a small bowl and leave to cool. When the sauce is cold, stir in the chopped garlic and chiles.

Barbecue the marinated chicken for about 5 minutes on each side, or until cooked through.

Arrange the chicken on a platter and serve with the bowl of sauce.

Nutritional value per serving:

Calories: 238

Fats: 8g

Carbohydrates: 20g

Salt: 2.38g

Saturated fat: 1.7g

Fiber: 0.4g

lamb kebabs with tzatziki

2lb lean shoulder or leg of lamb

Marinade

1¼ cups plain yogurt

1 teaspoon ground coriander

1 teaspoon ground cumin

¼ teaspoon freshly-ground pepper

juice of ½ lemon

Tzatziki

1 crisp cucumber, peeled and cut
   into ⅛-¼in dice

1-2 garlic cloves, crushed

a dash of white wine vinegar or lemon juice

1¾ cups reduced-fat Greek yogurt or best
   quality plain yogurt

1 heaped tablespoon mint, freshly chopped

sugar, salt and freshly-ground pepper

Mix the marinade ingredients. Cut the meat into 1in cubes, season with salt and pepper and put into the marinade for 1 hour at least.

Put the cucumber dice into a strainer, sprinkle with salt and allow to drain for about 30 minutes. Dry the cucumber on paper towels, put into a bowl and mix with the garlic, vinegar or lemon juice, and yogurt. Stir in the mint and taste. It may need seasoning with salt, pepper, and a little sugar.

Drain the meat and thread onto metal skewers or kebab sticks. Broil for 7-10 minutes over a barbecue, turning and basting with the marinade two or three times, serve with a green salad and tzatziki.

Nutritional value per serving:

Calories: 235

Fats: 12g

Carbohydrates: 4g

Salt: 0.64g

Saturated fat: 6.2g

Fiber: 0.3g

trimmed lamb cutlets with salsa verde & olives

24 lamb cutlets

olive oil, for brushing

rosemary sprigs and lemon slices, to garnish
   (optional)

Salsa verde

1 garlic clove

5 anchovy fillets

1 teaspoon capers

bunch of mint, finely chopped

bunch of flat-leaf parsley, finely chopped

1 teaspoon Dijon mustard

1 tablespoon red wine vinegar

6 tablespoons olive oil

salt and freshly-ground black pepper

Olives

2 cups pitted olives

bunch of rosemary

juice of 1 lemon

a little olive oil

Nutritional value per cutlet:

Calories: 123

Fats: 9g

Carbohydrates: 0g

Salt: 0.73g

Saturated fat: 3g

Fiber: 0.3g

First make the salsa verde: finely chop together the garlic, anchovies, and capers, place in a large bowl and mix together to a paste. Add the chopped mint and parsley, mustard and vinegar. Stir together and, as you stir, slowly add the olive oil. Once this is all mixed in, season and chill.

Slice the olives, put them in a bowl and mix in the rosemary, lemon juice, a touch of oil, and salt and pepper.

Place the chops on the barbecue and brush them with olive oil. Grill the chops for about 3 minutes on each side.

Remove and place on a large warmed dish with the bone facing outwards like a handle. Dress all the chops with the olives, followed by the salsa verde.

TIP

Generally, lamb chops are sold from the butchers in racks of about 6 cutlets. You can ask your butcher to cut them – you want your racks cut into cutlets with all the fat trimmed off. Alternatively, if you're going to cook a lot of cutlets, pre-order the number you'd like.

baked **potatoes** with dill & yogurt sauce

16 large 'old' potatoes

Dill and yogurt sauce
1$^3/_4$ cups sour cream
2 teaspoons Dijon or grainy mustard
$^3/_4$ cup plain yogurt
6 tablespoons fresh dill, chopped
$^1/_2$ teaspoon salt
sugar to taste

Scrub the potatoes well, prick them in 3 or 4 places with the tip of a knife. Wrap them in aluminum foil and bury in the hot coals of a barbecue for 45-60 minutes. Meanwhile mix all the ingredients together for the sauce. To serve, cut a cross in the top of each potato and spoon in some dill and yogurt sauce.

TIP

Of course these potatoes can equally be baked in a hot oven, but the flavor of potatoes cooked in coals is just so delicious that it is worth the bother.

Nutritional value per serving:
Calories: 202
Fats: 6g
Carbohydrates: 33g
Salt: 0.29g
Saturated fat: 3.6g
Fiber: 2.4g

black bean, corn, & roasted red bell pepper salad

1½ cups dried black beans

1 garlic clove

dried chipolte chiles

1 large onion, halved

1 cup long grain rice

1 tablespoon olive oil

8oz cooked corn (about 4 ears)

2 sweet red bell peppers, roasted, peeled, pitted and diced

2 tablespoons fresh cilantro or mint

2 tablespoons fresh parsley

6 scallions, chopped

Dressing

¼ cup red wine vinegar

2 tablespoons lemon juice, freshly squeezed

1 clove garlic, crushed

1½ teaspoons toasted and ground cumin seed

½ teaspoon toasted and ground coriander

¾ cup olive oil

Nutritional value per serving:

Calories: 583

Fats: 31g

Carbohydrates: 64g

Salt: 0.07g

Saturated fat: 4.5g

Fiber: 6.1g

Soak the beans in cold water for at least 3 hours or overnight. Next day drain them and place in a large saucepan with the garlic, chiles and onion. Cover with fresh water and bring to a boil. Continue to simmer for 1-1½ hours or until the beans are tender. Meanwhile, make the dressing by whisking all the ingredients together in a jar. When the beans are tender but still intact, remove the onion, garlic, and chiles. Drain and toss in the dressing while still warm. While the beans are cooking, cook the rice also: bring a large saucepan of water to a boil, add salt and the rice and bring back to a boil for 5-10 minutes or until the rice is tender. Drain and toss in the olive oil. In a large bowl, mix the beans with the rice, corn, red bell peppers, cilantro or mint, parsley and spring onions, and more dressing. Taste and correct seasoning if necessary.

How to roast and peel bell peppers

Preheat the oven to 475°F. Put the bell peppers on a baking sheet and bake for 20-30 minutes until they are soft and blistered. Place in a bowl and cover with plastic wrap. Leave to cool. Peel the bell peppers and remove the pips but do not wash them.

salads
&
sides

eggplant and cilantro dip

1 large eggplant

1 garlic clove, crushed

$1/2$ teaspoon sea salt

$1/4$ teaspoon ground black pepper

$1/4$ teaspoon ground cumin

2 dessertspoons extra virgin olive oil

1 tablespoon chopped cilantro

Preheat the oven to 375°F.

Bake the eggplant whole with the stalk left on for 40 minutes, or until the skin has browned and it feels very soft to touch. Leave to cool, then peel.

Place all the other ingredients except the cilantro in a blender or food processor along with the eggplant flesh, and blend until smooth. Stir the cilantro into the mixture and serve with flat bread.

Nutritional value per serving:

Calories: 117

Fats: 10g

Carbohydrates: 5g

Salt: 1.26g

Saturated fat: 1.3g

Fiber: 4.1g

deviled plums

1lb plums, pitted and diced

3-4 scallions, chopped with their green

1 teaspoon honey

juice of 1 lime

1 red or green chile, pitted and
finely chopped

Toss the diced plums with the scallions, dress with honey and lime juice, and finish with a sprinkling of chopped chile.

TIP

Serve this tart little relish with bean dishes.

Nutritional value per serving:

Calories: 44

Fats: 0g

Carbohydrates: 11g

Salt: 0.01g

Saturated fat: 0g

Fiber: 1.8g

date and **blood orange** salad

juice of 1 lime and 2 lemons

grated rind of $^1/_2$ lime and 1 lemon

$^3/_4$ teaspoon ground cinnamon

1 teaspoon orange flower water

2 tablespoons superfine sugar

4 blood oranges, peeled and thickly sliced

12 fresh dates, halved, stoned and cut into strips

pinch of *ras-el-hanout* (see TIP)

Put the lime and lemon juice and rind in a bowl, add a pinch of the cinnamon, plus the orange flower water and sugar and mix well. Leave for 1 hour at room temperature. Place in a saucepan and boil for 5 minutes to form a light syrup. Remove from the heat and leave to cool, then chill.

Place the orange slices and dates in a bowl and pour over the chilled syrup. Sprinkle over the ras-el-hanout, sprinkle over the remaining cinnamon to taste, and serve.

TIP

Ras-el-hanout is a North African spice mix made up of some 30 different spices, including dried roses, cardamom, turmeric, and cloves. Look for it in Middle Eastern stores and specialist food stores.

How to peel and slice citrus fruit

Cut the top and bottom off the fruit, then stand on one end and cut slices downwards to remove the peel and pith. Turn the fruit on to its side and cut into slices.

Nutritional value per serving:

Calories: 184

Fats: 0g

Carbohydrates: 45g

Salt: 0.04g

Saturated fat: 0g

Fiber: 4g

marinated broiled vegetables

Marinade

1 tablespoon extra-virgin olive oil

1 tablespoon balsamic vinegar

1 teaspoon honey

2 teaspoons lemon juice

salt and freshly-ground black pepper

1 eggplant, sliced into $\frac{1}{2}$in rounds

1 red bell pepper, cut in half lengthways, cored
   and pitted

1 red onion, sliced lengthways

2 zucchini, sliced lengthways $\frac{1}{4}$in thick

6 cherry tomatoes

4 asparagus spears, trimmed

small handful of oregano, chopped

small handful of basil, chopped

small handful of parsley, chopped

$\frac{1}{2}$ 14oz can kidney beans, drained and rinsed

Mix the marinade ingredients and reserve.

Place the vegetables under a high broiler until they begin to blacken and are soft. The red bell pepper should be cooked skin-side up. Remove from the heat and allow to cool. Peel off the red bell pepper skin and cut into strips. Place the vegetables in a bowl. Add the herbs and beans to the bowl. Pour over the marinade and mix well. Leave to marinate for 1-2 hours.

TIP

Make double the quantity and serve this dish as a main course, accompanied by rice, cous cous or cornmeal.

This dish is high in iron, fibre, and folic acid, as well as Vitamins A, B6, and C.

Nutritional value per serving:

Calories: 240

Fats: 8g

Carbohydrates: 33g

Salt: 1.17g

Saturated fat: 0.9g

Fiber: 11.9g

wok-fried choi sum with shiitake and tamari

5 cups (about 1lb) choi sum
   (Chinese flowering cabbage)

2 tablespoons groundnut oil

1 garlic clove, crushed

1 tablespoon finely chopped fresh gingerroot

4oz shiitake mushrooms

3oz fresh or canned Chinese water chestnuts,
   peeled and thinly sliced

1/3 cup chicken broth

2 tablespoons cornstarch

2 tablespoons tamari (or dark soy sauce)

1 tablespoon sesame oil

1 tablespoon roasted peanuts

Separate the stems from the leaves of the choi sum and cut them into pieces 2in long. Blanch the stems in boiling salted water until just tender, then drain well.

Heat a wok or deep skillet, add the groundnut oil, garlic, ginger, choi sum stems, mushrooms, and water chestnuts and stir-fry for 3–4 minutes. Add the choi sum leaves and cook for a minute longer.

Blend the broth with the cornstarch to form a paste and stir it into the pan. Stir in the tamari and sesame oil and toss well together. The sauce should form a glaze around the vegetables. Sprinkle over the peanuts and serve immediately.

Nutritional value per serving:

Calories: 158

Fats: 10g

Carbohydrates: 13g

Salt: 2.13g

Saturated fat: 1.7g

Fiber: 0.2g

baked onion with carrot & cumin sauce

10 x 10oz round white onions

unscented vegetable oil

6 cups vegetable broth

2$^3/_4$ cups bulgur (cracked wheat)

2 tablespoons olive oil

1lb 2oz corn kernels, cooked

2 cups pine nuts

8 plum tomatoes, peeled, pitted, and diced

$^1/_4$ cup flat-leaf parsley, chopped

$^1/_4$ cup fresh mint, chopped

juice of 1 lime

salt and freshly-ground black pepper

Carrot & cumin sauce

unscented vegetable oil

3 shallots, sliced

1$^1/_2$ teaspoons cumin seeds

1lb 8oz carrots, chopped

1 garlic clove, chopped

1$^1/_4$ cups white wine

4 cups vegetable broth

Nutritional value per serving:

Calories: 423

Fats: 15g

Carbohydrates: 55g

Salt: 1.5g

Saturated fat: 2.2g

Fiber: 4.7g

Preheat the oven 350°F. Line baking sheets with non-stick paper. Remove the outer skins of the onions, leaving the root and stalk intact. Cut the top off the onion to create a lid. Scoop out the middle using a spoon or melon-baller. Brush the insides with unscented vegetable oil and season. Place on the baking sheets in the oven and bake for about 20-25 minutes. Remove and leave to cool. Pour the broth into a large saucepan and bring to a boil. Reduce the heat, then add the cracked wheat and simmer for about 15-20 minutes, or until all the broth is absorbed. Add the olive oil and stir. Add the corn kernels, pine nuts, tomatoes, herbs, and lime juice; stir well and season. Fill the prepared onions with the mixture and replace the onion lids.

Heat a little unscented vegetable oil in a saucepan. Add the shallots, cumin, carrots, and garlic; sauté for about 3-4 minutes. Pour in the white wine and reduce by half. Add the vegetable broth, bring to a boil and simmer for 20-25 minutes. Season, remove from the heat and allow to cool slightly. Blend until smooth and pass through a fine strainer.

Cover the onions loosely with aluminum foil and place in the oven for 8-10 minutes. When cooked, place an onion in the center of each plate, pour on the sauce, and serve.

TIP

If you can get hold of Vidalia onions for this recipe use them – they are so sweet and delicious.

SERVES 4-6

PREPARATION TIME: 10 MINUTES

COOKING TIME: 40 MINUTES

button sprouts with parmesan and pearl onions

3 tablespoons olive oil

20 small pearl onions, blanched and peeled

1 tablespoon light brown sugar

3 tablespoons unsalted butter

3/4 cup meat broth

12oz button sprouts (baby Brussels sprouts)

2 tablespoons freshly-grated Parmesan cheese

salt and freshly-ground black pepper

Heat the oil in a skillet in which the onions will fit in a single layer, add the onions and cook over a high heat until golden all over. Add the sugar and half the butter and cook until the onions are caramelized, about 8–10 minutes. Pour in the broth and cook until it has evaporated.

Meanwhile, cook the Brussels sprouts in boiling salted water until just tender but still retaining a little bite. Drain them well.

In a separate saucepan, heat the remaining butter until foaming, add the sprouts and sauté for 5 minutes, until golden. Add the onions and toss together, then season with salt and pepper, and transfer to a serving dish. Sprinkle with the Parmesan and toss to coat.

TIP

Brussels sprouts are a strange vegetable, inspiring either love or hate. Here are some great ways of serving them:

• Tossed with roasted chestnuts and celery

• Puréed and finished simply with nutmeg and butter

• Mixed with reduced-fat sour cream and seasoned with a little curry powder

Nutritional value per serving:

Calories: 242

Fats: 19g

Carbohydrates: 12g

Salt: 0.57g

Saturated fat: 7.5g

Fiber: 4.3g

carrots and **beetroot** with north african spices

12 very small beetroot

4 tablespoons olive oil

6 carrots, cut into slices $^1/_2$in thick

$^1/_2$ stick unsalted butter

$^1/_4$ teaspoon ground coriander

$^1/_4$ teaspoon cumin seeds

$^1/_4$ teaspoon ground cinnamon

1 teaspoon lemon rind

1 teaspoon light brown sugar

pinch of saffron strands, soaked in 2
    tablespoons hot water for 10 minutes

1 teaspoon finely chopped cilantro root
    (well washed), if available

1 tablespoon chopped fresh mint

salt and freshly-ground black pepper

Preheat the oven to 375°F. Wash and trim the beetroot, leaving 1in of the top attached, but do not peel. Place in a shallow baking dish, pour over the oil, then cover with aluminum foil and bake until tender when pierced with a small knife, about 40-50 minutes. Uncover and leave to cool for 15 minutes, then peel them and cut in half vertically. Cook the carrots in boiling salted water until just tender, then drain and refresh under cold running water. Melt the butter in a large skillet, add the spices, lemon rind, sugar and saffron and cook for 1 minute. Add the beetroot and carrots and the cilantro root, if using, and toss together gently. Season to taste, transfer to a serving dish and sprinkle over the mint before serving.

How to pare lemons

Paring the rind of lemons or other citrus fruits is simple if you use a small tool called, believe it or not, a rinder. This removes fine strands of peel but leaves the pith intact so it doesn't taste bitter.

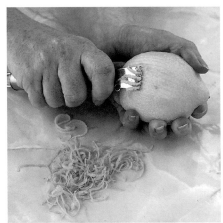

Nutritional value per serving:

Calories: 270

Fats: 22g

Carbohydrates: 17g

Salt: 0.44g

Saturated fat: 8.1g

Fiber: 4.4g

red bean salad with artichokes

2 cups cooked red kidney beans (canned is fine)

6 artichoke hearts, sliced

lemon juice

1–2 fresh chorizos, sliced

2–3 tablespoons olive oil

1 red onion, finely sliced into half-moons (see page 144)

1 tablespoon crumbled or chopped oregano

salt

Trim, scrape, and slice the artichokes. Cook in a little water for 10-15 minutes until the vegetables soften. Stir in the beans, reheat, and leave to cool.

When you're ready to serve, fry the chorizo slices in the oil until caramelized and crisp – don't let them burn. Pour the contents of the pan onto the beans, salt lightly and finish with lemon juice, onion, and oregano.

TIP

Pencas, the rosettes of a wild artichoke, a member of the thistle family and one of the first wild vegetables of spring in some parts of the world, can also be used in this recipe.

Nutritional value per serving:

Calories: 244

Fats: 11g

Carbohydrates: 25g

Salt: 1.88g

Saturated fat: 2.6g

Fiber: 8.4g

saffron-braised potatoes with paprika

4 tablespoons olive oil

10-12 (about 1lb 8oz) new potatoes,
   lightly scraped

3 garlic cloves, crushed

1 tablespoon tomato passata

1 tablespoon coriander seeds

$^{1}/_{2}$ teaspoon hot Spanish paprika

good pinch of saffron strands

3 cups well-flavored boiling chicken broth

1 tablespoon chopped fresh cilantro

salt

Heat the olive oil in a wide saucepan with a lid. Add the potatoes and sauté for 2-3 minutes without letting them color. Add the garlic and cook for a minute longer, then stir in the passata, coriander seeds, paprika, and saffron. Add a little salt, then pour on the boiling broth, cover and simmer for 30 minutes, until the potatoes are tender. Raise the heat and boil until the liquid has reduced to a thick sauce, turning the potatoes occasionally. Sprinkle with the cilantro and serve hot.

TIP

This dish can also be served cold as a first course or salad.

Nutritional value per serving:

Calories: 247

Fats: 12g

Carbohydrates: 31g

Salt: 0.94g

Saturated fat: 1.5g

Fiber: 2g

rice and vegetable timbale

1 large carrot, trimmed, peeled, and grated

1 mouli (white radish), trimmed, peeled, and grated

$^1/_2$ celery root, trimmed, peeled, and grated

2 beetroots, trimmed, peeled, and grated

14oz cooked basmati rice

2 tablespoons finely chopped flat-leaf parsley

1 tablespoon finely snipped chives

$^3/_4$ cup raisins

2 tablespoons extra-virgin olive oil

8 whole chives

Mix the grated vegetables thoroughly with the cooked rice.

Add the parsley, snipped chives, raisins, and olive oil and stir again.

Firmly press the mixture into timbale pots and refrigerate for at least 1 hour before turning out.

Decorate with the whole chives.

Nutritional value per serving:

Calories: 296

Fats: 7g

Carbohydrates: 56g

Salt: 0.26g

Saturated fat: 1.2g

Fiber: 4.4g

rice and lentils with crispy **onions**

1½lb onions (about 4 onions), finely sliced
½ cup olive oil
4 cups water
1½ cups brown lentils
1½ cups long-grain rice
salt and freshly-ground pepper

Heat the oil in a sauté pan, add the onions, toss and cook until richly golden.

Bring the water to a boil, add the lentils and cook for 20 minutes. Add half the fried onions and the rice. Season with salt and pepper. Stir well. Cover and cook on a very low heat for about 20 minutes or until both rice and lentils are cooked. Taste and correct seasoning if necessary.

Meanwhile continue to cook the remaining onions in the sauté pan until crisp and caramelized. Serve the rice and lentils at room temperature decorated with the crispy onions.

How to cut onions into half moons

Cut the onion in half lengthways. Peel each half and place cut-side down on the chopping board. Cut into fine half circles.

Nutritional value per serving:

Calories: 488

Fats: 20g

Carbohydrates: 66g

Salt: 0.28g

Saturated fat: 2.7g

Fiber: 5.3g

cassava with garlic and lime

3lb cassava root, peeled and cut into chunks
   (see TIP)
4 tablespoons olive oil
4 cloves of garlic, crushed
4 tablespoons lemon or lime juice
salt

To finish
fresh cilantro, chopped
cassava chips

Boil the cassava chunks in salted water for about 30 minutes until soft – don't worry if they disintegrate at the edges. Drain thoroughly.

Meanwhile, in a small frying skillet, heat the oil and lightly fry the garlic to soften. Add the citrus juice and bubble up. Pour the dressing over the cassava chunks and finish with a dusting of chopped cilantro. Serve with cassava chips.

TIP
Cassava can often be found in Caribbean markets and in some supermarkets - its brown hairy skin is often waxed to protect it and to increase its shelf life. Make cassava chips by slicing the root very finely on a mandolin and deep-frying or microwaving.

Nutritional value per serving:
Calories: 426
Fats: 11g
Carbohydrates: 84g
Salt: 0.28g
Saturated fat: 1.6g
Fiber: 3.8g

double-baked sweet potatoes

2 large sweet potatoes
1 teaspoon extra-virgin olive oil
1 small onion, finely chopped
½ teaspoon ground cumin
½ teaspoon ground coriander
4-5 button mushrooms, chopped
dash of soy sauce, to taste
1 teaspoon dried oregano
sesame seeds

Preheat the oven to 375°F.

Bake the sweet potatoes whole for 40-50 minutes until soft.

Gently fry the onion for 5 minutes in the olive oil. Add the mushrooms and spices to the pan and fry for another 5 minutes. Add the oregano and soy sauce and remove from the heat.

Cut each sweet potato in half lengthways and gently scoop out the flesh, being careful not to tear the skin. Add the flesh to the onion mixture and mix together well, adding more soy sauce if you like.

Place the potato skins on a non-stick baking sheet and fill with the onion mixture. Sprinkle with a few sesame seeds. Bake in the centre of the oven for 20 minutes then serve immediately.

TIP
This dish is high in Vitamins A, C, and E, and is a good source of fiber.

Nutritional value per serving:
Calories: 213
Fats: 4g
Carbohydrates: 42g
Salt: 0.47g
Saturated fat: 0.7g
Fiber: 5.1g

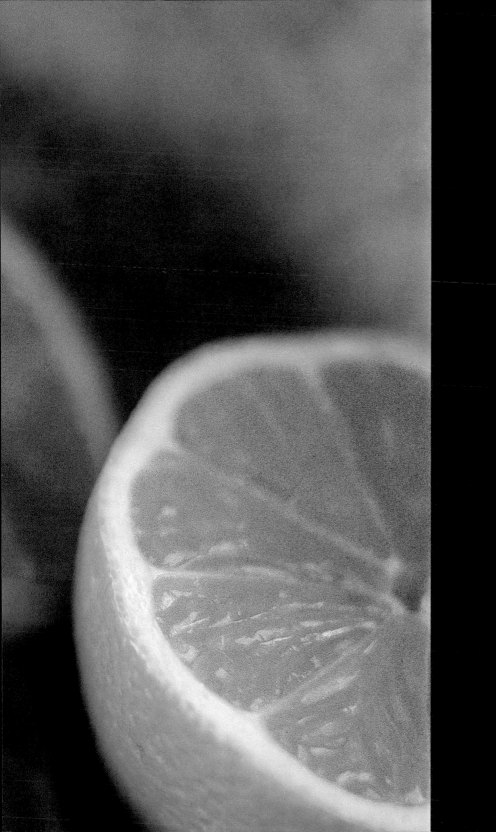

sweet
treats

spiced baked apples

2 cups golden raisins

1 cup brandy

1 teaspoon ground cinnamon

$^1/_2$ teaspoon ground allspice

1 cup light soft brown sugar

10 medium cooking apples

10 whole cloves

Place the golden raisins in an airtight jar, pour in the brandy and store in a cool, dry place until required.

Preheat the oven to 325°F.

Place the golden raisins in a bowl, then add the cinnamon, allspice, and sugar. Stir until combined. Core the apples, keeping them whole; do not peel them. Score the outsides around the middle. Place in an ovenproof dish, large enough that the apples will not touch – this allows them to cook evenly. Fill the apples halfway with the fruit mixture, place a clove in the center of each one, then fill to the top with the remaining fruit. Pour about $^1/_2$ cup cold water over the bottom of the dish, then bake the apples for about 45 minutes, or until they are soft and slightly puffed but still holding their shape.

Remove from the oven and leave to cool for about 5 minutes. Place each apple in a bowl and serve, pouring the syrup that collects at the bottom of the baking tray over the apples.

Nutritional value per serving:

Calories: 213

Fats: 0g

Carbohydrates: 42g

Salt: 0.03g

Saturated fat: 0.1g

Fiber: 2.2g

sweet potato purée

2 medium sweet potatoes, peeled and sliced

1½ cups superfine sugar

8 tablespoons water

1 orange, juice and rind

½ lemon, juice and rind

1 short stick cinnamon

1 tablespoon butter

2 eggs, separated

salt

To finish

cream

powdered cinnamon (optional)

few curls orange rind

Cook the potatoes until tender in enough lightly salted water to cover – they'll take about 40 minutes. Drain, allow to cool a little, and peel. Or bake in the oven and skin. Mash the flesh to a purée.

Meanwhile, melt the sugar in the water with the orange and lemon rind and juice and cinnamon, and bring to a boil. Simmer for 5 minutes and set aside. Remove the rind and cinnamon stick, and combine the hot syrup with the mashed sweet potato. Return the mixture to the heat and beat it with a wooden spoon until it thickens to a soft purée which holds its shape on the spoon.

Remove from the heat and beat in the butter. Allow to cool a little and beat in the egg yolks. Whisk the egg whites and fold them in. Allow to cool and pile into pretty glasses. Finish with a lick of cream, an optional sprinkle of powdered cinnamon and a few curls of orange rind.

TIP

This is often made with the white-fleshed sweet potato which, though less sweet than the orange-fleshed varieties, is considered to have a finer flavor. Either will do.

This pudding is a good source of Vitamins A, C, and E.

Nutritional value per serving:

Calories: 351

Fats: 6g

Carbohydrates: 76g

Salt: 0.36g

Saturated fat: 3.1g

Fiber: 1.5g

pink grapefruit and pomegranate sorbet

4 cups pink grapefruit juice
(about 10 grapefruit)
1 cup superfine sugar
1 egg white (optional)
1-2 pomegranates

Garnish
2 pink grapefruit cut into segments
pomegranate seeds
a little sugar
fresh mint leaves

Put the freshly squeezed grapefruit into a bowl, add the sugar and dissolve by stirring it into the juice. Taste. The juice should seem rather too sweet to drink: it will taste less sweet after freezing. Cut the pomegranates in half around the 'equator.' Open out and carefully flick the seeds into a bowl, discard the skin and all the yellow membrane.

Pour the mixture into the drum of an ice-cream maker or sorbetiere and freeze for 35-40 minutes. Fold in the pomegranate seeds. Scoop out and serve immediately or store in a covered bowl in the freezer until needed.

Before serving, chill the plates in a refrigerator or freezer. Then put 1-2 scoops of sorbet on chilled plate and garnish with a few segments of pink grapefruit. Sprinkle with pomegranate seeds, spoon a little grapefruit juice over the segments, decorate with fresh mint leaves and serve immediately.

TIP

For straight pink grapefruit sorbet, simply omit the pomegranate seeds.

Nutritional value per serving:
Calories: 355
Fats: 0g
Carbohydrates: 92g
Salt: 0.06g
Saturated fat: 0g
Fiber: 2.4g

coconut milk, yogurt, and red chile sorbet

1 small hot red chile

$2^1/_2$ cups superfine sugar

2 cups water

1 x 14fl oz can of unsweetened coconut milk

1 cup plain yogurt

4 tablespoons white rum

Cut the chile in half lengthways, remove the pips and dice very finely. Place in a saucepan with the sugar and water, bring to a boil and simmer for 1-$1^1/_2$ minutes or until the sugar has completely dissolved. Remove from the heat and stir in the coconut milk, yogurt, and rum. Leave to cool.

Pour into a sorbetière and freeze until firm, following the manufacturer's instructions. If you don't have a sorbetière, pour the mixture into a bowl and place in the freezer. After 30 minutes, when the mixture is beginning to set, remove it from the freezer and beat well with an electric beater or hand blender to disperse any ice crystals, then return it to the freezer. Repeat this two or three times, then leave until the sorbet is set firm.

TIP

In general, the smaller the chile, the hotter it is. Always buy chiles that are firm to the touch. Once they become soft, they lose their fresh flavor.

Nutritional value per serving:

Calories: 659

Fats: 11g

Carbohydrates: 137g

Salt: 0.42g

Saturated fat: 9.3g

Fiber: 0g

PREPARATION TIME: 20 MINUTES

CHILLING TIME: 12 HOURS

FREEZING TIME: 40 MINUTES

rose petal sorbet with summer fruits

4oz rose petals

2$\frac{1}{2}$ cups water

1 cup granulated sugar

rind and juice of 1 lemon

1 egg white (optional)

8oz summer fruits (strawberries, raspberries, blueberries, redcurrants, blackcurrants etc.)

Trim and discard the white part of the rose petals. Place the water and sugar in a saucepan and bring slowly to a boil ensuring the sugar has dissolved before boiling point is reached. Boil for 2 minutes then remove from the heat and add the rose petals, along with the lemon rind and juice. Stir well and leave to cool. Cover and chill overnight in the refrigerator.

The following day, pour the syrup through a strainer lined with a piece of damp cheesecloth. Reserve 6 dessertspoons of the syrup and set aside. Transfer the remainder to the bowl of an ice-cream maker and churn until frozen. If using the egg white, whisk it to soft peaks and add to the sorbet when semi frozen. Continue churning until completely frozen. Spoon into a chilled freezerproof container and freeze until required. Prepare the fruits according to their type. Divide between six tall glasses, add a dessertspoon of rose syrup to each glass and top with scoops of the sorbet. Serve at once.

TIP

Choose rose petals with a really sweet scent and a vibrant colour. Deep pink or crimson give excellent results. The best time to pick them is when the flowers are wide open, just before they start to fade.

Nutritional value per serving:

Calories: 142

Fats: 0g

Carbohydrates: 37g

Salt: 0.02g

Saturated fat: g

Fiber: 0.8g

watermelon crush

3/4 cup superfine sugar

1 cup water

2lb 4oz watermelon flesh (a 4lb 8oz melon
   yields approximately 2lb 4oz flesh)

juice of 1 lemon

Combine the sugar and water in a small saucepan and heat gently to dissolve the sugar. Increase the heat and boil for 2 minutes. Remove from the heat and cool.

Cut the melon into wedges, remove and discard the skin. Roughly cube the flesh, prising out the pips as you go. The handle of a teaspoon is a useful gadget for this.

In a food processor or blender mix the melon cubes with the sugar syrup and process to a smooth purée. Add lemon juice to taste.

Pour the mixture into an ice-cream maker or sorbetière and churn until frozen. If you don't have an ice-cream maker, pour the purée into a shallow container and freeze for 45 minutes to 1 hour. During this time ice crystals will start to form around the edges of the container. Remove it from the freezer and break up the crystals with a fork using a stirring and scraping action Return to the freezer and repeat every 45 minutes until you have a glistening mass of crystals. This can take 2-3 hours. Cover the container and freeze until required.

TIP

Serve within 1 to 2 days of making.

Nutritional value per serving:

Calories: 101

Fats: 0g

Carbohydrates: 25g

Salt: 0.01g

Saturated fat: 0g

Fiber: 0.1g

banana bread

3 large, very ripe bananas, skinned

4 tablespoons honey

2 medium eggs

1 stick butter, softened

1/2 cup light brown sugar

1³/₄ cups self-raising whole-wheat flour

1 level teaspoon baking powder

1 teaspoon freshly grated nutmeg

To finish

1 banana, skinned and quartered lengthways

Preheat the oven to 350°F. Butter and line a 9 x 6in loaf-pan with buttered greaseproof paper or butter paper.

Purée the bananas thoroughly with the honey and the eggs in the blender or food processor. Beat the butter with the sugar until light and white, then beat in the banana mixture, alternating with the flour sifted with the baking powder and spice, and blend thoroughly. Drop the mixture in the loaf-pan, spreading it well into the corners. Top with the finishing bananas.

Bake for an hour, until the cake is shrunk from the sides, well-risen and springy in the middle – it may need a little longer, in which case turn the oven down a notch and bake for another 10-15 minutes. Tip it out onto a baking rack to cool.

TIP

This bread is all the better for a few days in the tin so can be made well in advance.

Nutritional value per serving:

Calories: 487

Fats: 18g

Carbohydrates: 78g

Salt: 0.68g

Saturated fat: 10.3g

Fiber: 4.4g

banana and cashew slices

4 tablespoons sunflower oil

2 medium bananas, skinned

1/2 teaspoon vanilla essence

1 teaspoon ground cinnamon

1/4 teaspoon ground cardamom

1/2 cup cashew nuts

1/2 cup dessicated coconut

1/2 cup oats

1 apple, peeled and grated

Preheat the oven to 375°F.

Blend the oil, bananas, vanilla essence, cinnamon, and cardamom in a blender or food processor. Add the cashew nuts and blend for a few seconds to break them up.

Add the coconut, oats, and apple and blend for a few seconds more.

Turn into a greased 9in baking tray. Bake in the center of the oven for 25-30 minutes. Leave to cool, then cut into wedges.

Nutritional value per serving:

Calories: 185

Fats: 13g

Carbohydrates: 15g

Salt: 0.01g

Saturated fat: 4.5g

Fiber: 2.3g

carrot and dried fruit puddings

$2/3$ cup dates, diced

$3/4$ cup dried figs, diced

2 tablespoons stem ginger, diced

1 cup boiling water

$1/4$ cup raisins

$1/2$ teaspoon sodium bicarbonate

1 teaspoon baking powder

5 tablespoons unsalted butter

$1/3$ cup superfine sugar

2 free range eggs

$1^1/2$ cups self-raising flour, sifted

2 medium carrots, coarsely grated

$1/2$ teaspoon ground cinnamon

$1/2$ teaspoon ground mixed spice

Preheat the oven to 375°F. Put the dates, figs and ginger in a bowl, then stir in the boiling water, raisins, sodium bicarbonate and baking powder. Leave to stand for 15 minutes.

Beat the butter and sugar together until pale, then beat in the eggs one at a time. Fold in the flour, then stir in the dried fruit mixture, grated carrots and spices. Pour the mixture into six timbales or ramekins, 7fl oz in capacity, or into an 7in ovenproof dish. Place on a baking sheet and bake for 30-35 minutes for individual puddings or 40-45 minutes for one large one, until they are risen and golden and a knife inserted in the center comes out clean. Leave for 5 minutes before turning out.

Serve with heavy cream or fresh vanilla custard and a compote of dried fruits.

Nutritional value per serving:

Calories: 371

Fats: 12g

Carbohydrates: 64g

Salt: 0.94g

Saturated fat: 6.4g

Fiber: 3.8g

mixed berry corn muffins

2 cups rice flour

1¼ cups cornmeal

1½ teaspoons sodium bicarbonate

2 tablespoons soft brown sugar

9oz fresh or frozen mixed berries, such as
    cranberries, blueberries, blackberries,
    redcurrants or blackcurrants

1 dessert apple, cored, peeled, and grated

¾ cup yogurt

2 tablespoons lemon juice

1 tablespoon sunflower oil

⅔ cup unsweetened apple juice

Preheat the oven to 400°F.

Sift the rice flour, cornmeal, and sodium bicarbonate into a bowl. Add the sugar, berries, and apple, and mix well.

Mix the yogurt, lemon juice, oil, and apple juice in a jug, pour into the bowl and stir in to make a soft batter. You may need a little extra apple juice. It should easily spoon into a non-stick fairy cake baking tray, putting 1 spoonful into each case. You should have enough for 10-15 muffins.

Bake in the center of the oven for 15 minutes, or until golden. Leave to cool, then transfer to a wire rack.

TIP

These muffins freeze well. Make them well in advance then defrost and serve with warm with custard or sour cream.

Nutritional value per serving:

Calories: 188

Fats: 2g

Carbohydrates: 41g

Salt: 0.56g

Saturated fat: 0.4g

Fiber: 1.7g

index

acknowledgments

The publishers would like to thank the following authors for permission to use the recipes reproduced on the pages indicated: **Darina Allen**: 20, 42, 52, 94, 112, 116, 118, 144, 156; **Hugo Arnold**; 18, 40, 44, 66; **Ed Baines**; 68, 82, 102, 106, 114; **Aliza Baron-Cohen, Adrian Mercuri and Louisa J Walters**; 84, 122, 128, 148, 166, 170; **Vatcharin Bhumichitr**; 110; **Conrad Gallagher**: 14, 32, 48, 58, 64, 70, 80; **Paul Gayler**: 24, 26, 30, 74, 76, 98, 104, 126, 130, 134, 136, 140, 158, 168; **Elisabeth Luard**: 16, 34, 36, 46, 54, 56, 60, 88, 90, 92, 124, 138, 146, 154, 164; **Alison Price**; 22, 28, 38, 100, 132, 152; **Michael van Straten**; 78, 86, 142; **Mandy Wagstaff**; 160, 162; **Sarah Woodward**; 62, 72, 108.

The publishers would like to thank the following photographers for permission to use the images reproduced on the pages indicated: **Martin Brigdale**: 2, 12, 96, 111, 120; **Gus Filgate**: 15, 25, 31, 33, 49, 59, 63, 65, 69, 71, 73, 81, 83, 103, 107, 109, 115; 131, 135, 137, 141, 159, 169; **Georgia Glynn-Smith**; 1, 5, 7, 9, 50, 75, 77, 99, 105, 127, 150; **Jeremy Hopley**: 23, 29, 39, 101, 133, 153; **Francine Lawrence**: 17, 35, 37, 47, 55, 57, 61, 89, 91, 93, 139, 147, 155, 125, 165; **Ray Main**: 7, 18, 19, 21, 41, 43, 45, 53, 67, 79, 87, 95, 113, 117, 119, 126, 143, 145, 157; **Juliet Piddington**; 85, 123, 129, 149, 167, 171; **Jean-Luc Scotto**: 16, 22, 66, 72, 74, 84, 136, 144; **Sara Taylor**; 161, 163.